WELCOMING

Acknowledgements

I am thankful to the dear souls, past and present, of the First Baptist Church of the City of Trenton, New Jersey, who showed a newly minted seminarian what Christian hospitality looked like.

I am thankful to the brave souls of First Baptist Church, Scottsdale, Arizona, who are ready to venture down this road in order to build relationships with those on the margins of faith and the church. It is a privilege and honor to serve and journey with you.

I am thankful to KB, JG, AH, MH, KL, LM, and PV for their assistance in this work.

WELCOMING

A Church Guide to Demonstrate Biblical Truth in Love to LGBTQ Neighbors

James H. Coston

Welcoming by James H. Coston

ISBN: 978-1-59755-718-4

Published by: ADVANTAGE BOOKS™
Longwood, Florida, USA
www.advbookstore.com

Library of Congress Catalog Number: 2022951322

Name:	Coston, James H., Author
Title:	***Welcoming***
	James H. Coston
	Advantage Books, 2022
Identifiers:	ISBN Paperback: 9781597557184
Subjects:	Christian Books > Ministry & Evangelism
	Christian Books > Church Leadership > Pastoral Resources

First Printing: January 2023
23 24 25 26 27 28 10 9 8 7 6 5 4 3 2 1

Table of Contents

Introduction —Welcoming

Let me begin with a word of confession. In dealing with the issue of homosexuality and in ministering to gay persons, I have made mistakes. Lots of them. My words have not always communicated truth in love. My actions have not always mirrored those of Jesus. I am sorry. You will read of my previous fumbles when seeking to counsel friends struggling to reconcile sexual attraction and faith in Christ. As a minister of the Gospel of Jesus Christ, as a follower of the Triune God, as someone who proclaims God loves all sinners and seeks their redemption, I want to do better. I want to minister better. I want to follow Jesus better. And I want my church to proclaim and practice better. I want God's Church to proclaim and practice better.

You picked up this book because you want this too (I hope—if not, thanks for reading anyway). You have some questions and are seeking some answers regarding homosexuality, the bible, loving others. I share those questions. And I offer my answers here. These answers come through theological and biblical study. These answers come from 20+ years of pastoral ministry within several distinct congregations. These answers come after prayer, lament and personal confession.

God loves us. All of us. We are sinners who hurt others, ourselves and offend God. All of us. God wants to redeem us. All of us. One of the main conduits for communicating that love and redemption is the Body of Christ, the Church. All churches. So how do we tell others of love and redemption as God's church? How do we do this even when it is uncomfortable? How do we do this so the message is not lost in the method?

This book has a lofty goal—to detail a path for the Church/church to reach gay persons with the Gospel in a way that honors Jesus **and** those people Jesus died and rose from death to save. Followers will succeed or fail based on our ability, boldness and passion in WELCOMING others to Christ.

This book will challenge you. Depending on where you start on this issue, it may challenge you from different directions. Getting to this place theologically (thinking about God) and ecclesiologically (practicing thinking as a body of believers) has challenged me. It has challenged me to understand God's love as more than a list of do's and don'ts. It has challenged me to understand the Church as a place for broken people who do not measure up to God's holy standard. The Church/church is not a place for those who have fixed themselves [leaving aside a discussion of the inability for us to actually fix ourselves]. It has challenged me to welcome others to Christ because of this Truth. Therefore believers must open the doors of each church to everyone.

This doesn't mean that everyone will enter those doors. It doesn't mean all who are welcomed will reply to that invitation. But if the doors are shut, or locked, or barricaded, no one will enter. So we open the doors wide to others. And we welcome. And Jesus works His love.

The core of this practice for believers is Christian welcome. When disciples open the doors wide and invite fallen people into the embrace of God, they do so from a personal narrative of a changed life. Therefore we welcome others into the embrace of God so they too may have a changed life through the power of the Son of God—Jesus Christ. It is welcoming others in the name of Jesus. If you want some answers as to how to do this personally and communally, continue reading.

Chapter One: Welcoming Conversations shares my personal and theological journey on this subject, including theological failures inherent to our churches that foster unwelcome environments.

Chapter Two: Welcoming Clarity addresses the need for articulate thought and practice in our churches. If our churches are unclear on the issue of homosexuality, if they have not talked through a hospitable ministry, then our church people will fail to articulate the Good News and instead live out that message in a cloudy, confused manner. This chapter asks some questions. How can a church with an identity based in Scripture welcome those whose behavior contradicts the norms of that community? How is hospitality extended to gay persons in truth and grace? What are the core elements, possibilities, and limits of that hospitality? How are evangelical churches showing this hospitality to gay persons?

Chapter Three: Welcoming Mission details the task of the Church. Jesus welcomed others to Himself. He charged His followers to do the same—welcome others to Jesus. God did not suggest that we spread the Gospel story of Jesus; God commanded it. If we do not take the Good News to the ends of the earth, i.e. to EVERYONE, then we are not following Jesus. The mission is to people, individuals, with names, faces, and stories. Our mission involves being in relationship. While this isn't a new take on Christian missiology, the Church has failed on so many levels to offer this to gay persons. In this chapter, I distinguish orientation and attraction from behavior and provide a biblical basis for this distinction. This chapter also provides rebuttals to some ecclesial and cultural affirmations of homosexual behavior, with some Doctrine of Creation and Doctrine of Redemption thrown in for good measure.

Chapter Four: Welcoming Word lays out a biblical and theological understanding of homosexuality according to Scripture. This includes orientation, covenant fidelity, procreation, and chastity. It will also present thoughts regarding progressive revelation, particularly in terms of previous era attitudes toward women in ministry and slavery. And finally, I will posit one's view of scripture determines one's position on homosexuality.

Chapter Five Welcoming Community will define Christian hospitality. It will also dig into the meaning of community. What defines a community? How does a community grow without mutating into something other than the community? Then I'll share some thoughts on how the church can offer hospitality to gay persons and welcome them into the embrace of Jesus.

Chapter Six Welcoming Porous Boundaries will present a picture of church hospitality by utilizing Miroslav Volf's *Exclusion and Embrace*, and his idea of porous boundaries. Porous boundaries provide outsiders entrance into an identifiable community while allowing for that community to add new people to itself. The boundaries provide coherence of the group around an identity while the porous nature enables others to join the group. How does this apply to congregations? How does this apply to gay persons? Read and find out.

Chapter Seven Welcoming Process will share my own work on moving ministers and believers into postures of welcoming gay persons through a better understanding of theology and practice. It will share qualitative data from this work and suggestions for implementation within your churches and communities of faith.

In the *Conclusion*, I will share my hopes for the Church and for gay persons. We have far to go. We have a Savior who has already made the journey from death to life. Through Him, we will get there.

A word about terminology is warranted. I choose to use the phrase *gay persons* when referring to people with same-sex attraction and/or people who engage in same-sex behavior. Many gay persons view the term *homosexual* as an impersonal and dehumanizing slur. Some of this is due to the impersonal nature of labels. Some is due to how these terms have been applied and appropriated by society and the Church.[1] I will use the term *homosexual* to describe same-sex attraction and/or same-sex behavior in a general sense.

It seems only appropriate to close the introduction with a word from scripture. In Revelation 2-3, Jesus speaks to the seven churches through letters. The first letter is to the church at Ephesus in Revelation 2:1-5. Unless otherwise noted, all scripture quotations come from the New International Version.

> ***To the angel of the church in Ephesus write: These are the words of him who holds the seven stars in his right hand and walks among the seven golden lampstands. [2] I know your deeds, your hard work and your perseverance. I know that you cannot tolerate wicked people, that you have tested those who claim to be apostles but are not, and have found them false. [3] You have persevered and have endured hardships for my name, and have not grown weary. [4] Yet I hold this against you: You have forsaken the love you had at first. [5] Consider how far you have fallen! Repent and do the things you did at first. If you do not repent, I will come to you and remove your lampstand from its place.***

---

[1] Gregory Coles, *Single Gay Christian: A Personal Journey of Faith and Sexual Identity* (Downer's Grove, IL: IVP, 2017), 69-70.

What was distinctive about Ephesus? The city had a large population by 1st century standards with around 500,000 people making Ephesus one of the largest cities in the Roman Empire. Ephesus had a temple to goddess Artemis; it is considered one of the wonders of the ancient world; as Acts 19 shares, the Ephesians were a little touchy about it. The tourism this temple produced through worshippers bolstered the city economy.

In the letter, Jesus commends the Ephesian believers for keeping pagan practices out of their church. No one is worshipping Artemis. These followers have made sacrifices, real sacrifices of relationships and economics, to hold to the truth of the Gospel. Jesus continues telling them they have forsaken their first love and because of this they stand in danger of Jesus removing their lampstand, which represents the light of the Gospel coming from the church. No lampstand, no light shining, no Jesus, no church.

What was the first love that the Ephesian church had forsaken? Loving people who didn't know Jesus. Out of fear of outsiders and practices sinners might bring into the church, the Ephesian congregation became rigid. They only let in perfect people. They only invited the right kind of people to their fellowship. Inviting in the wrong people could taint the church, bring in practices they don't want, or dilute their community. The Ephesian church had become far more worried about harming their internal community and keeping it pure than reaching others for Jesus. Their first love, spreading the Gospel, commanded them to welcome in non-believers, those who don't know J, and those who are not living rightly. Their worry about what outsiders would bring with them kept them from doing this. They effectively closed their doors to the pagan unbelievers of Ephesus.

It is a legitimate concern: how to hold onto the Gospel truth without losing love for those who don't know the Gospel. There are standards within the church, absolutely and of course. Jesus never says be unholy, act unholy, or behave so as to fit in with others. The Son of God calls us to live rightly, to speak plainly, and to love excessively; Jesus never lowered standards. He also made sure that people, sinners and tax collectors, prostitutes and outcasts, knew that God loved them. We as His followers have the same call. We don't lower our standards. The first love however, the core, is to love those Jesus loved. Jesus will bring the change; we bring the message of His love.

We are commissioned to tell everyone the same message—Jesus loves you and we welcome you into His house to hear good news. Our first love is Jesus. We don't lose our faith by loving other people, loving people Jesus loves. We can't say, "be like us, change yourself and then come into our midst." That's backwards. The early church said come into our midst, be changed, and through Jesus become like us. Jesus transforms. How can we then exclude people who need transformation? This is our first love. Our churches can't be like Ephesus, which lived by the truth but without love. If we act like Ephesus, we will lose our light and our lampstand.

Later in the chapter there is the letter to the church at Pergamum in Revelation 2:12-16.

> ***"To the angel of the church in Pergamum write: These are the words of him who has the sharp, double-edged sword. [13] I know where you live—where Satan has his throne. Yet you remain true to my name. You did not renounce your faith in me, not even in the days of Antipas, my faithful witness, who was put to death in your city—where Satan lives. [14] Nevertheless, I have a few things against you: There are some among you who hold to the teaching of Balaam, who taught Balak to entice the Israelites to sin so that they ate food sacrificed to idols and committed sexual immorality. [15] Likewise, you also have those who hold to the teaching of the Nicolaitans. [16] Repent therefore! Otherwise, I will soon come to you and will fight against them with the sword of my mouth.***

Pergamum had very prominent temples with the Roman Caesar as the object of worship. Jesus mentions the martyr pastor Antipas who was killed for his faith there. The Pergamum congregation had the opposite problem to that of Ephesus. The Pergamum church welcomed everyone into its midst. They flung the doors wide open and ushered pagans, idolators and sinners inside. However, Pergamum accommodated the surrounding culture so much so that they looked exactly like everyone else. There was no discernible difference in how they lived or acted from the non-Christians.

Jesus reminds them of the double-edged sword; this represents the Word of God. The Word of God offers hope to sinners while it also, per 2 Timothy 3:16, teaches, rebukes, corrects and trains in righteousness those who believe.

Pergamum was great at welcoming people into its doors. But the invitation was not an invitation to change or be made new through the transformative power of Jesus. They invited people in and that was that. Come as you are and stay as you are. The references to the teachings of Balaam and the Nicolaitans refers to this. That isn't the Good News. Jesus invites us to Himself to free us, redeem us, transform, and remake us. I came to Jesus because I wanted my brokenness fixed.

The Pergamum church had to hold to its call to live a changed life through Jesus. That meant having standards. That meant not every societal practice was godly. It meant speaking truth in love to a pagan society. Great welcome. Great job loving others. Also speak truth in love.

With Ephesus and Pergamum as typologies, we have many of our churches. They are either too rigid to love the LGBTQ community into the arms of Jesus or too lax to speak the truth to the LGBTQ community that God calls each of them to live within specific boundaries of righteousness and holiness.

For decades, Ephesian churches and preachers have laid societal decline upon the LGBTQ community, told them that God hates them, called them abominations, pedophiles and driven them out of our churches. We have focused on six verses which clearly do prohibit same-sex intimacy; they are specific and undeniable in their condemnation of same-sex behavior. We have focused on six verses while ignoring the wider, larger, repetitive and more expansive biblical mandate to reach out to sinners, to those who don't know Jesus, and to the lost. There are a lot of people who are lost specifically because the Church has not gone out to find them, like a lost sheep, a lost coin, or a lost son (Luke 15) that no one carried to look for. Not caring to look for the lost, when Jesus wants us to go out and look, is itself sinful. A significant percentage of the LGBTQ community grew up in church and were treated so poorly they left and haven't darkened the doors of God's house since. We are called to love.

In the same way, Pergamum-like churches bless same-sex unions, bless polyamorous relationships, call them reflections of God's covenant, and ignore the biblical warrant to change and transform. This placebo gospel doesn't save, doesn't heal, and doesn't transform. My calling something wrong right doesn't make it so. We are called to speak truth of the Gospel.

We can't be Ephesus with its rigid boundaries. We can't be Pergamum without any boundaries. The rub with the two premises is how to fit them together, speaking the truth in love, so that we are neither Pergamum nor Ephesus but are the Church of Jesus Christ. How can the church speak the truth that homosexual practice is outside God's Will **and** seek out gay persons so as to invite them into a relationship with Jesus Christ? We as Jesus followers are called to biblical truth. We cannot water down a call to repentance or live a life worthy of the Son of God. We as Jesus followers are called to love others especially those who don't know Jesus. We cannot water down our mission to them. How do we maintain these two premises, how do we practically do this well, and how do we proclaim truth in love to the LGBTQ community?

That is what this book is about.

Study Questions

1. Share an experience you have had with a gay person where you did not offer hospitality or welcome.
2. How did this make you feel?
3. How did this impact the gay person?
4. How would Jesus have handled this?
5. What are the dangers of Ephesian rigid attitude?
6. What are the dangers of Pergamum's lax attitude?
7. How would you like to change your interaction in the future?
8. Pray for this person by name, and for other gay people you know by name. Pray they may come to know Jesus fully. Pray that Christ will use you to bring them to Himself.

Chapter One

Welcoming Conversations

I looked into the face of gay struggle at T.J.'s Deli in Winston-Salem, North Carolina, my senior year of college. I was having dinner with D., a friend since our freshman year at college. As we began to eat, he said he needed to share something with me. His voice sounded odd; D. was typically confident in his tone and demeanor. His hands began to visibly tremble. His face went ashen. He looked away as if to find some distraction from the immediacy of the moment. Mustering his composure, he finally said, "I'm gay." He then looked at me with his head facing the table but with his eyes up, as though peeking from behind his hair to gauge my reaction. He had braced himself for an anticipated hostile response. Did he expect me to scream at him? Did he expect me to get up from my meal disgusted and walk out? Did he expect me to condemn him? By the time D. had confessed this to me, he had endured each of these responses from former friends the week before.

I didn't scream at him. I didn't get up from the table and walk out. I didn't condemn him. I can't tell you exactly what I did say. I didn't know what to say. I did thank him for his courage in sharing this; I affirmed our friendship; I may have told him I would pray for him. And we continued to talk about his news.

We remained friends. We remain friends.

I knew personally then as I know today the church, my church, lacks a great response to confessions of this type. D. knew this at a far more visceral level than I do or ever will. Certainly his situation was not a singular occurrence. I think of G. who became a close friend of my wife in seminary. He came out during this time, confiding in my wife first and later in me. By this time my response had undergone some polish. I replied to his confession, "Theologically, I wish you weren't. But we are friends and will always be friends." I think of T. who I had the privilege of pastoring for a decade. He shared his profound loneliness, his desire to have a family with children and deep regret his faith would never condone his lifestyle. He knew the struggle of living for Jesus and having urges to love someone of the same sex. I can continue with similar stories.

Given you are reading these words, I suspect you have had similar experiences. You may have a family member who is gay. A child or sibling. You may have a neighbor who is gay. You may have co-workers who are gay. You may have all of these relationships and more in your life. You may wonder how to love these people well; how to speak the truth in a way that brings light, not heat; how to share in their struggles as you point the way to the Savior.

Or you may be like D., G., or T. You may be gay. If so, let me tell you with all the confidence I have in my soul Jesus Christ loves you. Jesus Christ died for you. Jesus Christ offers you eternal life that begins TODAY and therefore has something for you outside of same-sex intimate physicality. The church of Jesus Christ has done you a grave disservice. We have treated you as a faceless group. We have thrown our fears onto you. We have vacillated between the false pillars of condemning you and ignoring you.

Forgive us. We failed in our mission. We have shamed our Lord.

Please don't give up on Jesus, and please don't give up on the church or His followers. Jesus wants to embrace you, have you as a follower, and part of His Church.

I have firm convictions as to the biblical witness on homosexuality: homosexual behavior is outside God's Will. Christianity has had one voice on this from its inception, excepting the past three decades of North American Protestant Christianity. The prohibition of homosexual behavior precedes Christianity, extending to Judaic roots by millennia. Biblically and theologically, there is no basis to affirm homosexual behavior.

Paul says in Romans 3:23: *for all have sinned and fall short of the glory of God.* He writes in like sentiment in Romans 7:19-20: *For I do not do the good I want to do, but the evil I do not want to do—this I keep on doing. Now if I do what I do not want to do, it is no longer I who do it, but it is sin living in me that does it.* We all sin, believers and non-believers. I have had the blessing to grow in my discipleship within a faith community that accepted me as a sinner while encouraging my progressive sanctification. The church welcomed me before I became a believer; once having accepted Christ as my personal savior, it helped form me. My local congregation admonished me, challenged me and encouraged me. They wanted more for me; they wanted me to become more Christ-like.

What about gay persons? Do they have in like manner an invitation into the church? Does the church show gay persons hospitality so as to foster a climate of transformation whereby they may encounter Jesus and grow in holiness to become Christ-like?

I've heard arguments gay people shouldn't be in the church until they stop being homosexual. I've heard professing believers say those people will be welcome once they change. If salvation is found in Jesus, we cannot expect people to solve their own sins first and then come to worship as pristine people. That's not the Gospel.

My first call was to a church in Trenton, NJ, that had an illustrious history. It also had some history it bore with regret. I was told for a time in the mid-20th century, a pair of Deacons stationed themselves at the entrance to the church, looking over every person who approached the doors. I was told that if those Deacons did not approve of one's appearance [I don't know if this meant dress or skin color frankly], they would tell that person to go home. Could anything be farther from the Good News of Jesus than this? In sharing that tale, I heard the relief of the congregation in that they now opened the doors to everyone.

If you have closed the doors of your church--or the doors of your heart--to gay people, you have sinned. Repent. Jesus needs you loving others so others will come to Him through your welcome. Jesus needs you loving others so you can experience His love fully.

The Bible has also challenged me to take seriously its placement of boundaries. Scripture offers a lot of sexual boundaries and these boundaries include the exclusion of same-sex behavior. So as to provide a semblance of comprehensiveness, sex outside of marriage is sin; adultery is sin; lust and lustful practices are sin. I've heard arguments scripture is unclear on homosexual behavior. I have heard people say love is love and God doesn't care. Love misused, misdirected, mis-purposed is not love. It is sentimental expediency. It is not sacrificial, deep-seated, care for others.

Rob Bell wrote a book titled *Love Wins* in 2011. The theme is a loving God would not exclude anyone from that love. The book sounds good. It makes for a catchy bumper sticker. But it fails. Love without truth isn't real love. Love without truth is a placebo. *Redemption Wins* would make a better book title, theme and/or bumper sticker. God loves us and that love seeks most to redeem us—all of us, including those with same-sex urges and desires. And redemption is hard won, hard fought and often painful. The giver of redemption—the Son of God who died on the cross—knows this. Receivers of redemption know this too. Change is hard. Extinguishing old habits and cultivating new ones is hard. Leaving one community and becoming part of another is hard. The love of Jesus doesn't seek to validate us as we are; the love of Jesus seeks to redeem us from who we are to become who God intends us to be.

Jesus calls the Church—embodied by every church—to welcome sinners by speaking the truth and love of the Gospel. That's the mission.

I know in my deepest soul that D., G., and T., as well as others have all prayed earnest prayers to God as they struggled with their libidinous urges. I have witnessed the ways in which each loves Jesus. I have seen each serve others from a place of sacrificial love following Christ. They believe in forgiveness, the power of redemption, righteousness and grace. In some ways, their understanding of those words may go to a far greater depth than my own.

Our baptisms are eschatological cures for our sinfulness, but they are not ontic cures for our transgressions. The sacrifice of Jesus Christ justified believers before God. The road to becoming Christ-like still lies in front of believers. Post-baptism, I have sinful struggles. And these believing gay Christians have their sinful struggles. I am blessed my own battles are not fought publicly, which is not the case for most gay persons. Whether owing to Puritanical roots or other reasons, sexual sins garner more public derision and castigation than other sins. How might Christian community grow were it to offer loving correction and counsel rather than condemnation and exclusion to those within the church who struggle?

[2] Many evangelical churches have failed to welcome gay persons because they have little to offer as an alternative other than prayers for God to miraculously change attractions—and for God to do so without their/church involvement. The evangelical church has failed to articulate a theology of singlehood. It has failed to articulate a theology of sexuality, other than to tell youth to wait until after the wedding to have sex and, post nuptials, suddenly what had been characterized as dirty and sinful will become beautiful and pure. So we are left to say to gay persons, "Get fixed. Then come join us even though we don't have ways to minister to you or paths of discipleship for you to explore in community." Not a great offer. Not what Jesus offers.

The idol of family has in many pulpits replaced the demands of the Triune God. Scripture advocates, accepts and affirms singleness (1 Corinthians 7:8), but pulpits don't preach this. Our churches have so promoted the idea there is a man for every woman and a woman for every man we do not know what to do with singles, other than to try to get them married. This anthropology has provided fuel for divorce and remarriage,

---

[2] David Garland, *1 Corinthians* (Grand Rapids: Baker Academic, 2003), 236-238. 1 Corinthians 6:18 delineates sexual sins from other sins. David Garland offers interpretations of this verse to explain Paul's setting apart sexual sins from other transgressions. One concerns the qualitative difference between sexual sins and non-sexual sins. Sexual sin inflicts more harm upon the sexual sinner than does other sin. The sexual harm includes physical, psychological and spiritual effects.

Another interpretation notes a qualitative difference between sexual and non-sexual sins. Sexual sin leaves a lasting effect upon the person. This effect is both spiritual and personal. Joining the body into a physically sinful union damages that person's spiritual union with Christ. Sexual sin also damages personal relationships through objectification of others and the reflective objectification of the self.

A third interpretation disassociates sexual sin because of the unique nature of sexual union and intimate physical contact. While gluttony and drunkenness harm the physical body, sexual sin unites the body in an offensive way with sin above and beyond the ways that food and alcohol may corrupt the body. Sexual union involves a greater degree of intimacy and connection than do other sins. The misuse of this uniting is therefore a greater offense.

which the church has come to accept because it can do little else [picking and choosing which sins to focus upon, perhaps?]. Without a theology that properly articulates sexual practice, without a theology that views singleness as a viable and divinely ordained alternative to marriage, then the church cannot speak with theological adequacy to gay persons.

And yet, the witness of Jesus Christ and my evangelical nature tell me the church is the place in which to hear of the good news, repent and receive forgiveness; thereafter we seek to live in the grace of God. This path applies to gay individuals as it applies to all individuals. However, few Bible-believing churches welcome gay persons into their midst. For all of our evangelical talk of liberation from sin, some have not only failed to declare the Gospel to gay persons but openly fomented hostility towards them. Jesus welcomed sinners into his arms; many of his followers have pushed these sinners away from church doors. This must change both for the sake of those struggling with gay attraction and for the sake of the new community which Acts 2 ushered forth on Pentecost two millennia ago.

There are some churches whose sexual ethics contradict scripture and Christian tradition. Within much of Protestant Christendom, these churches are denoted as Welcoming and Affirming. They affirm homosexual behavior. This leads many to affirm a great deal of other sexual behavior. I know of a congregation that grew so tired of dialogue, debate and having to read uncomfortable passages aloud they stopped doing so. Over time, their sexual ethic became, "Do whatever feels good as long as you honor the other person, and it's all consensual." Now that has changed to "other persons" with the rise of polygamy in our society. One of their members left her husband to engage in a lesbian relationship. This leaving took the form of co-parenting their small child for a time. This endeavor without deeper bonds of mutual love and fidelity was bound to fail; and so they got divorced shortly thereafter. The church celebrated this person for throwing off an inauthentic sexual relationship [great euphemism for breaking up a family] and becoming her true self, neglecting the damage done to the former husband, the young child who has dealt with rapid and primary changes, and the breaking of a marital covenant.

What message does this send to young people who have hormonal changes and new feelings? What does it offer its adults who struggle with lust and fidelity? Does the commitment of marriage matter?

Churches of this ilk have basically closed the words of God to this part of our humanity. If God doesn't have something to say about such an important part of my personhood—my sexuality—then why should I bother with the other stuff God may have to say?! And if God is nothing more than a great-therapist-in-the-sky, I can find therapy somewhere else.

Some churches and denominations affirm homosexual behavior. Some justify this through a myopic reading of scripture. Some rely upon a hermeneutic of progressive revelation allowing each reader to dismiss untenable and challenging portions of the Bible. Some reject Jewish and Christian tradition. Some do this out of penitent guilt for Christian sins against gay persons. Rather than preach transformation, their Gospel is reduced to inclusion, tolerance and stasis. Their Gospel amounts to "come and remain as you are" rather than Jesus' proclamation to *repent, for the Kingdom of Heaven has come near* (Matthew 3:2).

This "welcoming and affirming" approach doesn't offer healing; rather it compounds the pain of gay persons. Jesus did not open wide His arms so that His embrace would freeze us as we are. Jesus embraced us that we might be forever changed and molded into His followers. The Gospel is about new life, not a continuation of our old lives. When Jesus calls us into community, He calls us to transformation. This redemptive metamorphosis works toward healing our mental, emotional, spiritual, physical and sexual selves.

Before we can reimagine our ministry to gay persons, we have to rethink our welcome to gay persons. To do so, we have to have conversations. We have to talk. We have to share. Conversations are dialogical, not monological. They are a back and forth, giving and receiving. There is a divine ratio of speaking to listening—one mouth and two ears—that we must honor. The first step to welcoming gay persons to Jesus is to welcome conversations.

Our conversations won't be perfect. They won't be flawless. They may be frightening or confusing or scary, at first. Your willingness—your church's willingness—to welcome conversations displays a faith and trust in God the Holy Spirit to move and touch hearts. The first step is to welcome conversations with gay persons on their experiences, their seeking after God, and their struggle in society.

You know gay people. They are in your life either as neighbors, friends, co-workers, or family. Talk to them. Ask them about their lives. Listen. The initial step to welcoming someone into the embrace of the Savior of the World is to listen to their stories. Really listen. Ask questions. Be curious. Hear what they share. Build a relationship, if you don't already have one. The person sitting across from you is a person that Jesus loves. The person staring at your face is a person Jesus died for. The person talking to you is someone Jesus wants. So welcome conversations!

Study Questions

1. Share your experiences with gay persons in your family, community, workplace?
2. Share about an uncomfortable situation when you didn't know what to say or do relating to a gay person?
3. How might they have felt uncomfortable?
4. In what ways does the Church [or your church] **explicitly** tell gay persons to go somewhere else?
5. In what ways does the Church [or your church] **implicitly** tell gay persons to go somewhere else?
6. If you were gay, would you find your church a safe, welcoming place?
7. Does the invitation to receive Jesus extend to gay persons?

Chapter Two

Welcoming Clarity

God calls the Church to speak truth and grace, to warn of disobedience and its consequences, and to welcome the lost into His embrace and Christian fellowship. Churches do all this through the telling of the story of Jesus Christ. That story provides followers with boundaries to pursue a path of holiness. The Bible prohibits homosexual behavior in both the Old and New Testaments. The Bible also mandates followers of Jesus to welcome sinners into his presence. These two statements are not mutually exclusive. They go together.

How do these biblical tenets co-exist? How can evangelical churches take the Bible seriously—in both its prohibitions and directives—to show hospitality to gay persons in a manner that both upholds the truth of the Gospel and invites gay persons to encounter the transformative love of Jesus Christ? What practices have evangelical churches undertaken to welcome gay persons into their congregations? Are there limits to that welcoming? If so what are those limits? How may a congregation offer hospitality to gay persons in such a way as to bring those individuals—and couples—into a relationship with Jesus Christ that excludes tacit and/or active acceptance of homosexual behavior? Most of our church leaders don't have ready answers for this. If the leaders cannot articulate a position, then most of our church members can't either. It is a hard topic. If Jesus loves sinners, and if Jesus calls believes to welcome sinners to experience Him, then Jesus expects His Church to do the same!

As stated in the introduction, this is not an academic exercise. This is about the lost who Jesus wants in relationship with Himself; and the Church is Jesus' primary instrument to welcome those same people into that relationship. How do we do that while maintaining integrity to the call for believers to be holy, to live differently, to exhibit the Kingdom of God? I wanted to find out. So I started asking some questions.

In 2017, as I began working on the dissertation that served as the foundation of this book, I began talking to Lead Pastors. I asked them to share their church's position on homosexuality; how their church arrived at that position; and how this position had been communicated internally and externally to the congregation. I thank each and every one for sharing with me honestly and candidly. These were some hard conversations.

I asked, *How did your church arrive at this position?* Here are a sample of answers: "*Fighting—firing the pastor—living in factions.*" Another commented, "*[w]ith pain and many departures;*" "*[b]lood, sweat, and tears.*" Two confessed to intentionally ignoring this issue and avoiding it. A pastor of a neighboring church, and personal friend, shared, "*We are intentionally ambiguous.*" He and his leadership did not want to get into the issue, because he knew it would make some people mad and others sad, no matter what their conclusion was. So they avoided it as long as they could, even while parishioners asked questions. That path did not end well for my friend or his church. They are now a Welcoming and Affirming church; and in my humble opinion, they lack the vitality and urgency they once possessed to reach others for Christ. They also lack the leadership of my friend who is no longer there. Only a small percentage could relay their churches had undertaken intentional study of the issue to come to a unified church understanding on homosexuality. If church leadership doesn't have a clear position on homosexuality then how can their churches?

If the church's position isn't clear, then the church cannot communicate clearly in explaining that position to its members. Some pastors I spoke with had communicated their church position from the pulpit and through church documents and/or policies members could access. But those who had undertaken this communication admitted this was monological—here is what we believe and it does not need additional comment. They did not have discussion or dialogue on this position and frankly, confessionally, said they didn't want to. Without internal cohesion on a position, how can a church communicate its position to outsiders, and how does it have a theology and practice of witness if there is a hole concerning sharing the

Gospel with a specific set of the population? Poor communication, or a lack of communication, has a cascade effect that damages everything.

In these conversations with other pastors, my final question was *What has been the greatest difficulty within your congregation surrounding homosexuality?* This elicited a number of intriguing and forthright responses. Many shared their primary difficulty was in educating the congregation theologically so they could welcome gay persons without that welcome being construed as an acceptance of homosexual behavior. One friend shared, "*[c]oming from a Bible conservative position, the hardest thing has been to convince the church that accepting the tension between welcoming gays while not condoning their sexual preference is what we believe Jesus and the apostles command.*" Another said, "*[a]greeing that it's a sin like any other—especially greed, obesity, pride and lying—and realizing that people change after they become disciples not before.*" Still another, "*[w]e are a fairly small church and I think part of the struggle has been proper training on the struggle of what a person that wants to follow Christ but has homosexual tendencies or is homosexual goes through.*" A final word on this aspect of church struggle, one pastor noted the most difficult hurdle was "*[e]stablishing we were all sinners, once we accepted that fact it was easy to allow everyone else in.*"

These church leaders want to provide safe space within which to discuss the theological and ecclesiological implications of homosexuality and hospitality. One pastor shared a need of "*[l]etting people know it is safe to share their fears and concerns.*" But wanting to do this within a congregation was easier than actually achieving this space, per the words of another pastor who expressed the need of, "*[h]aving a conversation that does not devolve into cable news. I have to teach my congregation how to have a theological conversation. They...also could learn to handle conflict better.*"

The experience of other churches going down the road of discussing homosexuality can lead others to a place of reticence. A lead pastor/friend almost killed his church by going into this issue without setting markers for safe discussion. He preached on one of the Pauline passages that speaks of homosexuality. His sermon made passing reference to homosexuality because the text did and then his message moved on to his main points, which had nothing to do with homosexuality. The congregation heard his passing reference. They wanted to know how he came to this conclusion and if that was the position of the church. Caught off guard, he hastily called for some church discussion. Having failed to set prior parameters for that discussion, the back and forth among the congregation soon got away from him. Side conversations proliferated. Those conversations didn't remain in that church but spread to parishioners of others churches and to leaders of others churches so many within the community learned of this discord. I myself heard about this episode from congregants, peers, and friends. Congregants wanted to bring in outsider speakers. Members produced position papers on this and distributed them; I received one. Things went sideways SO FAST. It took the better part of 18 months for the congregation to come to a definitive understanding. During those 18 months, this issue sucked up all the energy of this church. Some members left the church over the process. Some left over the final position. My friend survived in his role as Lead Pastor, but there was cost professionally, personally, and congregationally.

Suppose a church has the conversation and suppose that conversation yields a position on homosexuality. How then does the church live that out with gay persons? Some lead pastors spoke of the need for boundaries within their church polity. Among these were concerns of "*[w]hen and how to draw the line of involvement of homosexuals*" and "*[m]aintaining the balance that anyone struggling with lusts/pornography and sex outside of marriage is all the same, regardless the specifics of each one.*" Another shared, "*[w]here lines are drawn for acceptance into the church and leadership. Other sins are often cited to 'equalize' non-celibate gay acceptance into the church and in leadership positions.*"

A final comment sums up both the opportunity and the challenge for the Church. One pastor shared, "*[w]e have a large portion of the congregation who believes it's [members who are homosexual or engage in homosexual behavior] not at our church. They enjoy living in denial rather than having the challenging conversations. The topic is not just a theology issue, it is present and real and comes with lives. Denial cannot work.*" Amen.

Our churches lack clarity. The conversations demonstrated to me that churches don't understand what they believe and therefore cannot articulate that belief. I firmly believe what we understand becomes what we speak, which becomes what we do. If we don't know what we think about homosexuality, then we don't know how to talk about homosexuality, and we don't know how to act as Jesus followers with gay persons.

Churchclarity.org begin in October 2017. It began with the mission to chronicle local church stances on LGBTQ+ people through a scoring system. They have since taken to scoring other policies but the organization originated on the issue of homosexuality. From its website:

> ***Church Clarity is a crowd-sourced database of local congregations that we score based on how clearly they communicate their actively enforced policies. Our mission is to increase the standard of clarity throughout the Church Industry. We are not advocating for policy changes; we are standardizing church policy disclosure, whatever the policy or type of church in question. People deserve to know the truth.***

Church Clarity does not officially advocate for policy changes. However, their stance on this issue is not hard to discern; they are 'inclusive, affirming and celebrating of all people' according to their website. *Affirming* is church lingo meaning that a congregation affirms homosexuality behavior as right, proper and within God's Will. *Welcoming and Affirming* has long been code for this [obviously, I make a distinction between the call to welcome and the affirmation of homosexual behavior so keep reading]. Church Clarity began as a way to shame non-LGBTQ+ affirming churches by exposing those churches to the wider culture that has embraced sexuality and sexual expression without boundaries. Good things can come out of poor motivations, however.

Church Clarity pushes for pastors, lay leaders, churches, and followers of Jesus to know what they believe. This organization put that need on the web for all to see. Within the pews, our people need clarity. What does the Bible say about this issue? How do believers relate to gay persons, faithfully and lovingly? What mission do we have as followers of Jesus to gay persons? We need to know what we think, how to share that and how to behave as a result. Church Clarity has this right: clarity is reasonable. It is more than reasonable; clarity is vital.

As the pastor above said, *Denial won't work.* This is not an issue to avoid. These are not people to ignore. Jesus didn't shy away from hard tasks. Think of his continual dining with sinners to the chagrin and anger of the Pharisees. Think of his initiating a conversation with a Samaritan woman. Think of the Cross. As His followers, we cannot hide from this. But we need clarity. Having clarity as a goal is easy; getting to clarity is tough. And it is a hard path to get to a position of clarity. But congratulations, you have in your hands a book that clarifies this for your church. There is a blueprint that has worked; I know firsthand.

As God's people and God's Church, we welcome conversations. We welcome clarity as it comes to belief and practice. We welcome God's Word to provide that clarity to us. And we welcome God's mission to everyone.

Study Questions

1. What is your church's position on homosexuality and church involvement by gay persons?
2. How has your church communicated this within the church and the larger community?
3. How could your church and/or church leadership offer more clarity on this?
4. How would clarity impact you?
5. How would clarity impact your church?
6. How would clarity impact your larger community?
7. How would clarity impact gay persons?
8. Pray God will deliver or continue to provide clarity for your church and its leadership.

Chapter Three

Welcoming Mission

I remember my ordination well. It was a Sunday evening service at West End Baptist Church in Columbia, Tennessee. I had finished seminary; the First Baptist Church of the City of Trenton, New Jersey, had called me into leadership.

Baptist ordinations vary. My own was…less than thorough [my interns past and present are likely wondering why their own ordinations contained far more rigor and examination than my own did]. I had contacted church members from my hometown in early spring, informed them of my graduation and installation at First Trenton in early summer and after some conversation about my education and work, we scheduled a visit to Columbia and an ordination service.

After preaching at West End that morning in the summer of 1998, I met with the Deacons for examination. I sat in a seat with the Deacons semi-circling me and answered biblical, theological and practical questions for an hour. After passing that examination, they held an ordination service. There was a tight schedule for the examination. There was the start of the ordination service coinciding with the arrival of refreshments for the fellowship following the ordination service. Theoretically, I could have failed in my preaching that morning or in my answers to the questions that afternoon and brought the proceedings to a screeching halt. But, in hindsight, I think I would have had to have failed miserably. I gather that I didn't.

The biggest moment in the ordination service happens at the laying on of hands. Here, ministers and deacons touch the ordination candidate and often say a few words of encouragement or wisdom privately. It is a biblical symbol imparting responsibility and authority. That action made an impact on me.

However, it was the sermon of the executive minister of West End's local ministerium that resonated with me. That message continues to speak to me decades later. I heard the challenge to have a *heart for sinners*. Having a heart for sinners meant caring for fallen people, loving people who may not always be lovable, ministering to the broken and hurting. It is having compassion for those who need, from the stranger to the congregant to the person I see in the mirror.

Having a heart for sinners doesn't sound like a new or revolutionary concept, right?! Jesus had a heart for sinners. But hearing this mandate as someone who would lead a church and speak to others with an authoritative voice was like hearing this Gospel with new ears. God loves all people, not just the people who would fill the church I would lead. My work is to affect those in the pews. My work is to affect those who don't know Jesus, who may act in ways that offend or surprise, who may be different or downtrodden, and who will never ever sit in one of these pews.

That charge to this soon-to-be ordained minister was to maintain within my person and ministry a heart for sinners. This is the mission Jesus gave to His followers. The words of that association minister impacted me then and have remained in the forefront of my ministry ever since.

I believe in the Great Commission that closes Matthew's Gospel: Matthew 25:18-20 [my translation]

> ***18 Then Jesus came to them and said, "All authority in heaven and on earth has been given to me. 19 As you go, make disciples of all nations, baptizing them in the name of the Father and of the Son and of the Holy Spirit, 20 and teaching them to obey everything I have commanded you. And surely I am with you always, to the very end of the age."***

Knowing the grace of Jesus Christ personally is not the end of the process of God remaking each person. Jesus commands we disciples make new disciples through our proclamation of grace and truth and through our practice of that grace and truth. Jesus commands that we, who know the embrace of Jesus, go on mission and welcome others into His embrace.

I conceive of this commission using some established theological positions. These suppositions are not universal within Christendom. But if you are reading this book, you likely have some affinity for evangelical theology. The term *evangelical* has become a loaded term growing to encompass more than just biblical and theological truth. Before moving forward on the mission, let me define the evangelical presuppositions, and by exclusion disregard other expanded meanings.

First and primary, evangelical churches understand Creation and creatures fall under both the benevolent providence and terrifying judgment of a holy and righteous God.[3] We are sinners. We have earned death. And yet, God is active in the world seeking the redemption of creation and creatures through Jesus Christ the Son of God, the Word incarnate, the only and final atoning sacrifice for the sins of humanity (1 John 2:2).[4] Jesus is the Alpha and the Omega (Revelation 22:13), the Lamb of God (John 1:29), the Resurrection and the Life (John 1:29). Christianity confesses a living God who works for reconciliation, forgiveness and salvation. All because God loves sinners.

Second, the Bible has final authority over theology and practice for believers. The Bible is revealed and therefore supersedes reason, tradition and experience.[5] Furthermore, the hermeneutical task of interpretation rests upon the text of Scripture itself. In other words, the meaning of the Bible will come from the Bible. Readers necessarily bring their own subjectivity to the text; your own experiences and perspectives will impact how you understand biblical passages. However, the text itself offers a message that confronts and challenges readers. In reading the bible, we encounter a voice other than our own—that of the Holy Spirit.

Related to this, the Bible's revelation is normative for human behavior. God's Word transcends societal norms. Contemporary ethics and changes in cultural values do not determine the relevance of the Bible; rather, the Bible determines the relevance of those ethics and values.

Continuing, the Bible is inspired by the Holy Spirit (2 Peter 1:20-21). Transmission came through human agents; the Bible did not drop down

---

[3] Schmidt, *Straight & Narrow?*, 21.

[4] Thomas E. Schmidt, *Straight & Narrow? Compassion & Clarity in the Homosexuality Debate* (Downers Grove: IVP Books, 1995), 17.

[5] Ibid., 18-20.

from heaven in final form. And yet, God's Word directs readers—and hearers—toward God and the story of God dealing with God's creation from Adam and Eve through the early church. The message of the Bible has a unified coherence and relevance. The Bible testifies to Jesus Christ and presents his Good News to those seeking salvation as well as a path for those seeking to live as disciples of the Son of God. As John Webster states: "To say that Holy Scripture is the authoritative canon is to say this determinate collection of writings, received and read as a unified God-given prophetic and apostolic testimony, legitimately claims the acknowledgement, assent and obedience of the church and its theology."[6]

Let me add evangelical is a political term, in that Jesus cared about people and cities. The Greek word *polis* literally means city. That is the root for our word politics. However, the connection ends there.

Jesus was not a Republican. He was not a Democrat. He was not a Libertarian or Socialist or…whatever political party you are most interested in. Jesus made a strong contrast between politics of His day, whether Roman or Jewish, and did so to the profound disappointment of His followers, at least at first. Once they realized politics were much smaller than what Jesus was doing concerning the Kingdom of God, they stepped in line with their Savior and eschewed politics in favor of proclamation. As an evangelical, I eschew partisanship and political equivocation in favor of proclamation of the Kingdom of God.

The question of biblical authority directly impacts how a believer understands homosexuality. I accept the Bible as normative. I read it as having authority over my life. I understand it as divine revelation. God speaks through scripture. My theological understanding comes from the Bible. Scripture challenges and tests my thoughts and practices. If one accepts the Bible as normative, then one's understanding of homosexuality will have basis in the Bible. The evangelical church does not arrive at a position on homosexuality or hospitality through a study of situational ethics or focus groups; rather, Christians are to abide by God's Word as revelation (2 Timothy 3:16). We are bound to follow, and the Bible

---

[6] John Webster, *Holiness* (Grand Rapids: Eerdmans, 2003), 19.

presents the path upon which we are to follow. Obedience is a choice, but the path of faithfulness is clear and direct.

Finally, evangelical theology believes all people need to hear the Good News of Jesus, accept the free offer of salvation, and seek to live as disciples (Mark 16:15).[7] Evangelical churches accept the privilege and responsibility of the mission of directing others to Jesus through invitation and witness in word and deed. The church must reach outsiders with the Gospel however necessary to share the message of Christ. The mission of evangelical churches is therefore two-fold: to form disciples within the faith community and to lead those outside the church into a personal relationship with Jesus Christ. In living out this mission, believers and churches glorify God the Father, Son and Holy Spirit.

This is not an exhaustive outline; seeking to characterize and categorize evangelical churches would be a project in and of itself. However, for the purpose of this project, these points are salient: Jesus Christ is Lord and Savior (Romans 10:9); the Bible is the revealed Word of God and has authority over the followers of Jesus (1 Thessalonians 2:13); everyone needs the redemptive power of Jesus in their lives (Romans 6:23); and the church has a mission to spread the Good News of Jesus to others (Psalms 96:3).

All this evangelical garb points me to believe in my Savior and thereby have my faith expressed through love (Galatians 5:6). This expression comes through having a heart for sinners. Loving those who Jesus loved. Going to those who Jesus went to—those deemed by the "righteous" as sinners and unwanted; people that synagogue goers stayed away from and viewed as unclean. These are the people Jesus loved. Tax collectors. Prostitutes. Cheats. Thieves. Outsiders. Sinners. They are the people Jesus commands His disciples to love.

How did Jesus love the people the world had cast off? He welcomed them. He invited those on the margins into his company. He welcomed impure, diseased, broken souls. He offered redemption through relationship. He closed the doors to no one. He talked with and dined and

---

[7] Ibid., 21-22.

invited Himself into the homes of those in need. He spoke their names. He touched them. He related to them. And He sought them out specifically.

So, as believers in Jesus Christ, following God's Will as shared through scripture and the Holy Spirit, we have a directive to reach those who do not know Jesus. This is not an option. This is not a suggestion. This is not conditional. Reaching others with the Gospel is a mission. If we are disciples, we will commit to this mission with our whole hearts. And we will welcome this mission to gay persons.

With profound sadness and personal regret, many of us Jesus followers have not welcomed gay persons well—or at all. Rather than shining the light of Christ, we have wielded de-contextualized verses like cutting torches.

If you read the Gospels, Jesus had great skill with scripture. The folks who felt its sting were the religious officials and self-righteous Pharisees—those puffed up with self-assurance of their righteousness felt Jesus' wrath. Jesus showed compassion to the lost. To the self-righteous, Jesus displayed anger and rebuke. That warns me now; it should warn all of us. The Good News isn't meant to beat people down who need it. It is meant to be a lifeline, a course correction, a voice speaking into the void saying God loves you. How can we as believers provide guiding light instead of burning lasers?

For gay persons, their homosexual attraction can dominate and define their identities.[8] Reasons for this abound. Church rejection may lead to a greater identification with the root of that rejection. Likewise, our culture's obsession with sexuality has made sexual identification more primary. Personal situations of an injurious nature may lead gay persons to greater unity with other gay persons through shared experiences of rejection. For gay persons, their sexuality provides a uniqueness within the greater culture. In some cases, this unique marker may be flaunted; in other cases, it is hidden and covered.

---

[8] Andrew Marin, *Love is an Orientation: Elevating the Conversation with the Gay Community* (Downers Grove: IVP Books, 2009), 38.

Jesus said the worth of a person is not defined by that person's sexuality or sexual activity (John 8:1-11).[9] As human beings we are sexual beings; sexuality is a part of human makeup. But the Bible says we are much, much more than a collection of urges and hormones (John 1:12). Our sexuality does not encompass us fully. It does not define us before God. Likewise, our sexuality is not how we are primarily known or know others. There is much, much more to being human than just sexuality. This is a biblical view. This is a Gospel view.

As a believer, I understand God knows me fully, completely, comprehensively in ways beyond my own self-understanding. That same God offers me wholistic transformation through love, grace and redemption. While sexuality is a facet of personal humanity, our culture has inflated and stretched this singular aspect to cover the whole person so that one's sexuality has become a primary identifier of that person, or people, and a means to define that person or group. There is much more to consider in thinking of ourselves and others. We cannot deny sexuality is a part of our humanity; we cannot deny there are other parts as well.

Many believers have fallen into this societal trope. People who praise Jesus will cast slurs at gay people with the same lips. They label this group in the same way one would label adversaries or opponents. While many Christians decry outwardly the sexualization of society in its many forms, we have fallen under the influence in heightening sexuality. Society has positioned sex as the ultimate god; knowingly or not, many believers have indirectly done the same in their treatment of gay persons.

Jesus calls us to something greater as we have a heart for sinners and engage in mission. While Scripture prohibits homosexual behavior, it does not explicitly condemn homosexual attraction. This point does not have total agreement within bible-believing circles. There is agreement that engaging in homosexual behavior is sinful. Gay persons may live faithful, celibate lives in accordance with God's will [more on this to come]. The

---

[9] Loader, *Sexuality and the Jesus Tradition*, (Grand Rapids: Eerdmans, 2005), 45.

Bible rejects homosexual behavior; it does not explicitly reject those with homosexual attraction per se.[10]

Our culture, on the other hand, has taken a "born gay so it's ok" attitude. Welcoming and affirming churches have adopted this mantra. Some source this position within the doctrine of Creation. Since God made people with an attraction to members of the same sex then that attraction must be within God's purposed intention. Sexual desires are so deeply ingrained within human beings that they are involuntary. God would not have deliberately created creatures with a bent toward those desires if God considered acting upon those inherent desires unholy or wrong. These churches welcome gay persons into their midst and invite them to remain as they are, per this understanding of the doctrine of Creation.

This understanding confuses homosexual attraction and homosexual behavior. Homosexual attraction may be biological—a point neither proven nor disproven—making this a scientific issue. Homosexual behavior on the other hand is a thoroughly theological issue.[11] All humans have sexual thoughts and impulses that arise in a spontaneous manner. This evidences the Fall and our inherent sinfulness. Jesus preached dwelling on these thoughts and impulses is sinful; and certainly, following through on them is also sinful (Matthew 5:27-30).

Churches that welcome and affirm homosexual behavior falsely equate attraction and behavior, merging an urge with a practice.[12] Some argue that opposing a natural biological impulse, the attraction in this case, damages the self; gay persons should therefore engage in homosexual behavior rather than face waves of self-loathing by suppressing these urges. Denying one's natural desires results in inauthentic living and a denial of being who

---

[10] For arguments that homosexual orientation is inherently sinful see Denny Burk and Heath Lambert, *Transforming Homosexuality: What the Bible Says about Sexual Orientation and Change* (Phillipsburg, NJ: P&R Publishing, 2015). For a rebuttal on this point, see Nate Collins, *All but Invisible: Exploring Identity Questions at the Intersection of Faith, Gender and Sexuality* (Grand Rapids: Zondervan, 2017).

[11] Sprinkle, *People to Be Loved*, 130.

[12] Marin, *Love Is an Orientation*, 38.

one truly is.[13] This is the understanding of creation that supporters of homosexual behavior hold. This places human experience upon the throne of God.

Gay persons have worth. They have goodness. They matter. They are made in the image of God. But we are all sinners in need of redemption. Believers do not ultimately seek a good that exists within ourselves or creation; we seek something higher called holiness that is beyond the power of creation to grant. Experience is not the ultimate arbiter of right or wrong. Homosexual attraction and its behavioral extension of homosexual practice are not good simply because some people desire those experiences. They are not good because they appear natural. They are not good because they express who those people "authentically" are. Experience, natural urges, supposed authenticity do not supersede other criteria, including divine revelation and biblical mandates, to determine goodness or righteousness. One's nature does not determines one's morality. To say otherwise is to say that morality is individually based upon each person's experiences, authentic desires and natural impulses. This makes modification of one's desires and rebuke of subsequent behavior unjustifiable. Experience does not stand above God's revelation but rather serves that revelation, even to the point of being rejected in the face of revelation. Experience is not a master. God summons experience before his throne as a servant. Our experience, our natural impulses, our authentic desires all need redeeming and remaking. Experience offers creatures neither perfection nor holiness; those gifts come only from Jesus. God's revelation, inclusive of the biblical witness, alone serves as the basis for behavior and judgment (1 Corinthians 6:9-11).

The doctrine of creation does not stand on its own. It relates to the work of God thereafter, namely redemption through Jesus Christ. Creation has a *telos*, an end or purpose, which is Jesus Christ.[14] Jesus is the culmination

---

[13] Jonathan Grant, *Divine Sex: A Compelling Vision for Christian Relationships in a Hypersexualized Age* (Grand Rapids: Brazos Press, 2015), 142.

[14] Karl Barth, *Church Dogmatics III/1* (Edinburgh: T & T Clark, 1958), 24.

of creation. Jesus is the work of God to reconcile humanity.[15] Jesus is the atonement (Romans 3:21-25 and 1 John 2:1-2).

This understanding of creation presupposes a recognition of fallen humanity. As creation points toward Jesus, it points toward reconciliation. The doctrine of Creation elucidated by those affirming homosexual behavior fails to include a notion of sinful humanity or redemptive purpose. Present creation is not as God originally intended it. The world is broken and humanity is flawed (Romans 8:18-23). These defects affect every facet of humanity—mental, emotional, physical and spiritual. This depravity includes sexual attraction. Gay oriented sexuality is broken and flawed. Heterosexuality is broken and flawed.[16] All of humanity is broken and flawed (Romans 3:23). Peter in Acts 2:38 invites hearers to repent and be made new. Jesus himself called followers to come and be changed in Matthew 4:17. God did not arrive on earth incarnate to affirm humanity as it was. Rather God came in the flesh to redeem and remake humanity (2 Corinthians 5:17).[17]

Humanity's imperfection does not mean we as flawed creatures should accept and abide within our sinfulness, tacitly accommodating it.[18] While everyone's sexuality is broken, The Bible expressly prohibits homosexual behavior while promoting heterosexuality within marriage. Rather than leading to a stance of moral equivalence, the doctrine of redemption provides justification and a path toward sanctification for followers of Jesus.

---

[15] Karl Barth, *Church Dogmatics IV/1* (Eugene, OR: Wipf & Stock Publishers, 2001), 22.

[16] Coles, *Single Gay Christian*, 46 and 55. The life of faith provides a means for the justification and sanctification of broken sexuality within heterosexual marriage. Heterosexual marriage can redeem heterosexual attraction. Scripture affirms heterosexual attraction within heterosexual marriage. Neither homosexual attraction nor homosexual behavior are affirmed in Scripture.

[17] Jesus Christ, *vere deus, vere homo*, identifies with sinners. Jesus remains perfect and his sacrifice provides atonement for sinners through the crucifixion. As he identifies with sinners, his resurrection provides sinners with new life and transformation.

[18] For an argument along this line see David P. Gushee, *Changing Our Mind*, 2nd edition (Canton, MI: Read the Spirit Books, 2015).

That path of sanctification involves following biblical imperatives, not sinful impulses (Romans 6:1-4).

I do not know of a Christian leader who would advise an alcoholic to drink alcohol because the alcoholic desires it authentically and deeply. Who would advocate that heterosexuals have sex whenever hormonal desires arise simply because those desires arise? Does doing something in the name of authenticity justify such behavior? According to the biblical message, discipline defines our humanity more so than urges and desires, including parameters and boundaries for sexual expression and enactment (1 Timothy 4:6-10).[19] It does not follow that creation in its present form mirrors perfectly God's intentions for creation. This applies to all persons, not just gay persons. Becoming Christ-like involves rejecting those things that damage our relationship with Jesus. We do not find our true selves except through Christ dwelling within us (Ephesians 3:17).

The doctrine of redemption calls us away from our sinfulness as creatures into becoming new creations. That calling at the behest of Jesus in some ways bids us to die to ourselves. We take up our cross and follow Jesus, no matter where that may lead, no matter the cost, no matter what desires or impulses we must deny. In following Jesus, we come into something greater and more substantial than any reward a desire or impulse could deliver. We only become our true selves as Jesus takes us through His crucible of redemption and the Holy Spirit leads us to an ever-increasing union with the Redeemer. Momentary denial for the sake of discipleship leads to eternal fulfillment in the Kingdom of God in the present and the future.

Jesus presented an eschatological message of transformation. This eschatology is not fully realized. While the Kingdom of heaven has come near, it is also not yet (1 Corinthians 13:12). Jesus meets people where they are; he does not then leave them in their predicaments (Mark 2:17). To suggest otherwise is to preach a false Gospel. H. Richard Niebuhr's warned about this false Gospel: "A God without wrath brought men without sin

---

[19] Thomas Breidenthal, "Sanctifying Nearness," *Theology and Sexuality: Classic and Contemporary Readings*, ed. Eugene Rogers (Malden, MA: Blackwell Publishers, 2002), 352.

into a Kingdom without judgment through the ministrations of a Christ without a Cross."[20]

The doctrine of Creation, inclusive of human depravity, points toward a doctrine of Redemption. God accepts us into a divine embrace; God then transforms us, lifting us above and beyond our sinfulness.[21] This is the Gospel. Jesus died to save us from our sins. As believers justified through the crucifixion and resurrection of the Son of God, we travel a path of sanctification, being made holy as we become disciples of Jesus. Christ redeems us from our sins. This includes a redemption of our sexuality and, most importantly, our identity. The opposite of homosexual is not heterosexual; it is healed and whole.[22]

Scripture provides pathways by which sexuality may seek sanctification. One is marriage between a man and a woman. Within this covenant, spouses may freely offer themselves in complete vulnerability to one another. They may also freely accept the offer of the other in that same vulnerability. Another pathway is celibacy. Paul advocates for the latter, while allowing for the former in 1 Corinthians 7:7. The Bible does not offer alternatives outside of heterosexual marriage and celibacy.

While gay persons may hold as their primary identifier a homosexual attraction, salvation through Jesus transforms them into a new person.[23] Redemption transforms those who know the love of God. Jesus does not view his followers as homosexual or heterosexual. He does not view his followers as married or single. He views them as disciples.[24] This call to discipleship may involve leaving prior relationships (Luke 14:26); it may involve taking up new relationships (Acts 2:42-47). Disciples find peace and fulfillment through unity in Jesus Christ. They are remade, reborn, redeemed. This does not entail present perfection, utter absence of sin, or complete holiness; however, it entails Christ has repurposed each follower

---

[20] H. Richard Niebuhr, *The Kingdom of God in America* (Fishers, IN: Wesleyan, 1988), 193.

[21] Gagnon, *The Bible and Homosexual Practice*, 213.

[22] Marin, *Love is an Orientation*, 70.

[23] Sprinkle, *Two Views on Homosexuality*, 162.

[24] Grenz, *Welcoming but Not Affirming*, 105.

to live in submission to the will of God. "According to the Christian confession, the space in which human living is undertaken is created and reconciled space which is on the way to its final perfection."[25]

Let me illustrate my point in case it got lost in all the theological material in this chapter. We as Jesus followers are called to speak truth in love. Speaking truth without love is not what Jesus commanded. Loving without speaking truth is not what Jesus commanded. If you and/or your church are guilty of doing one of these without the other, you are not following Jesus. We must share the truth of the Gospel—Jesus loves you and wants more for you than a life without Him as Lord offers. We must love those who hear the Gospel in action, visible ways and extravagantly. These go together necessarily.

A friend of mine pastors a large Baptist church in the south. He shared with me the dilemma in getting this balance right. There was a lesbian teenager in that youth group. She was welcomed and included and invited to participate. He asked aloud, did we focus on the love part to such an extent that we failed to include the truth part? Some churches have the opposite problem—all truth without any love. How do churches get comfortable, or reside in a Jesus mandated discomfort, speaking the truth in love? We do this by understanding we have a mission to go to those who don't know Jesus. That mission says speak the truth in love—both at once. For those who personally know Jesus, this is a welcome mission.

Study Questions

1. How did believers show you love before you accepted Jesus as your savior?

2. Share an instance when you consciously and intentionally showed God's love to a non-believer through your actions. What happened because of this?

3. Share an instance when you didn't. What happened because of this?

---

[25] Webster, *Holiness*, 104.

4. How does your church love sinners?
5. How does it not?
6. How might my friend's church's youth group have spoken the truth in love to the young lesbian?
7. Pray for those close to you who don't know of Jesus' love for them. Commit to being the hands and feet of our Savior in demonstrating that love to them.

Chapter Four

Welcoming Word

I visited a church in North Carolina many years ago. I neared completion of seminary and made a summer trip south for some rest and relaxation. Someone introduced me to the pastor sharing with him that I attended Princeton Theological Seminary. Evidently, he was not a big fan of Princeton; he had some ties to a Baptist school in North Carolina I later learned. While I cannot verify this, I have thought since then that the opening of that service was directed my way. The pastor came onto the platform and asked everyone to hold their bibles up high and wave them around. He then said something quasi-idolatrous about scripture, revering it almost like a divine person, getting close to worship and adoration of it. If he didn't cross the line between replacing the Word of God with the words of God, he got awful close. I think he worried that Princeton had taken the Bible out of me so he thought he would try to reinsert it, or something along those lines [Princeton didn't take the Bible out of me by the way]. Or maybe he didn't want me to attend again; on that point he was successful as I have not darkened those doors since.

While I do not worship the Bible, it is an objective, revelatory gift from God. It is the message of God's story through history from creation to re-creation. Scripture points me to Jesus Christ. In this it tells me of salvation, discipleship, forgiveness and sacrifice. The Bible reassures me. The Bible confronts and challenges me. The Bible is normative for me. I do not debate the Bible's efficacy or inspiration. I take those for granted through the power of the Holy Spirit.

You don't need me to rehash the myriad of works exegeting the Bible on the issue of homosexuality, particularly the most direct verses.[26] My own interpretive practices assume the plain reading of Scripture in line with two millennia of Christian tradition and its far older Jewish roots. Instead in this chapter I share with you insights from my study on homosexuality within the biblical context and Christian tradition, as well as answers to arguments seeking to refute the Bible's stance and commands.

The biblical position on homosexual behavior is clear and without condition—homosexual behavior is prohibited and sinful.[27] This stance goes back to the origins of Judaism in its universal rejection of homosexual practice. Within the Holiness Code of Leviticus, homosexual behavior is considered a greater sin than incest and adultery and only exceeded in its degree of sinfulness by bestiality.[28] The Old Testament was not ambiguous in its denunciation of homosexuality (Leviticus 18:22 and 20:13).

For the New Testament homosexual behavior remains under the rubric of sexual sins. Both male-male relations and female-female relations are considered sinful and offensive to God while also dangerous to the faith community (Romans 1:26-27, 1 Corinthians 6:9 and 1 Timothy 1:10).[29] While Jesus did not explicitly comment on homosexuality, his comments on sexuality illustrate a very strict view on sexual holiness. Preston Sprinkle argues within the Jewish rabbinic tradition surrounding first

---

[26] The most direct verses on homosexuality are Genesis 19:1-29, Leviticus 18:22 and 20:13, Romans 1:26-27, 1 Corinthians 6:9 and 1 Timothy 1:10. For an exegesis of these, go to Appendix A.

[27] Preston Sprinkle, *People to Be Loved: Why Homosexuality is Not Just an Issue* (Grand Rapids: Zondervan, 2015), 70. See also Robert Gagnon, *The Bible and Homosexual Practice* (Nashville: Abingdon Press, 2002); Stanley Grenz, *Welcoming But Not Affirming* (Louisville: Westminster John Knox Press, 1998); and Richard Hays, *The Moral Vision of the New Testament* (San Francisco: Harper, 1996).

[28] Robert Gagnon and Dan Via, *Homosexuality and the Bible: Two Views* (Minneapolis: Augsburg Fortress, 2003), 48.

[29] Luke Timothy Johnson, "Disputed Questions: Debate and Discernment, Scripture and Spirit," *Theology and Sexuality: Classic and Contemporary Readings*, ed. Eugene Rogers (Malden, MA: Blackwell Publishers, 2002), 370.

century Judaism, Jesus favored the stringent sexual ethics of Jewish theologian Shammai over the more liberal understanding of Jewish theologian Hillel.[30] As homosexuality was considered a gentile (i.e. pagan) practice, neither rabbi commented upon homosexuality per se. In other sexual matters, the schools of Hillel and Shammai offered some diversity in the sexual and marital comportment of first century Judaism. Hillel allowed for a husband to divorce a wife for a multitude of reasons including the wife being a poor cook. Shammai only allowed for divorce in the event of the wife's infidelity. Shammai's school taught prohibitive and rigid understanding of sexual conduct. Jesus' strong statements regarding divorce (Matthew 19:1-12), adultery (John 8:1-11) and co-habitation (John 4:1-18) evidence a strict sexual ethic. Likewise Paul's direct comments on homosexual practice leave no doubt as to his position: homosexual behavior is sinful (Romans 1:26-27, 1 Corinthians 6:9 and 1 Timothy 1:10).[31]

What about homosexual orientation?

The Bible categorically defines homosexual behavior as sinful. As noted in Chapter Three, the Bible does not similarly define homosexual orientation. Orientation means a person has a predisposed attraction to one sex over the other. Men attracted to women and women attracted to men have a heterosexual orientation.

Regarding scripture and its tradition, some scholars have argued orientation as a category of understanding, whether heterosexual or homosexual, was a foreign concept in the first century. Therefore, based on this reasoning, Paul's point lacks force against an enlightened understanding now available to twenty-first century congregants. The idea being since Paul didn't know about orientation then, his views are incorrect and we can update them since we now know about orientation.

These scholars miss Paul's point. Neither Paul nor the Levitical Holiness Code address orientation specifically; they only address

---

[30] Sprinkle, *People to Be Loved*, 73.

[31] Robert Song, *Covenant and Calling: Towards a Theology of Same-Sex Relationships* (London: SCM Press, 2014), 71.

homosexual behavior.[32] Leviticus 18:22 and 20:13 denounce homosexual actions; they do not address inner desire or attitudes of attraction that may lead to homosexual actions. Paul also focuses on homosexual practice in 1 Corinthians 6:9 and 1 Timothy 1:10. The lone possible exception to this is Paul's writing in Romans 1:26-27 [for more on this, see Appendix A]. Homosexual orientation is neither condemned nor affirmed within the Bible.

Evidence shows that sexual orientation was a concept during Paul's lifetime.[33] Aristotle references homoerotic desires as being both acquired and inborn.[34] Soranus, a contemporary of Paul, argued homosexual orientation was a product of biology more so than environment in his work *De Morbis Chronicis*.[35] The concept of homosexual orientation was a category of sexuality in Paul's day. Even without that proof, Paul's reasoning for rejecting homosexual behavior does not stand upon an understanding of orientation or sexual identity; thus, the notion of orientation would have had no impact upon his denunciation of homosexual behavior.[36]

Isn't this really about monogamous relationships, heterosexual or homosexual?

Other arguments have emerged regarding the applicability of the Bible's witness on homosexuality. Specifically, would the existence of monogamous, faithful, committed gay relationships have an effect upon the force of the biblical witness against homosexual practice? A number of writers argue a union of two committed partners (male/male or female/female) mirrors covenantal theology making the genders of those

---

[32] Robert Gagnon, *The Bible and Homosexual Practice* (Nashville: Abingdon Press, 2002), 462.

[33] Sprinkle, *People to Be Loved*, 60.

[34] Aristotle, *Nicomachean Ethics,* trans. C. D. C. Reeve (Indianapolis: Hackett Publishing Co. Inc., 2014), 120.

[35] Thomas K. Hubbard, *Homosexuality in Greece and Rome: A Sourcebook of Basic Documents* (Berkeley: University of California Press, 2003), 463.

[36] William Loader, The *New Testament on Sexuality* (Grand Rapids: Eerdmans, 2012), 324.

partners superfluous.[37] God and Israel voluntarily entered into a covenant based upon mutual love and faithfulness (Deuteronomy 29). Marriage exhibits this mutual faithfulness. So the argument goes that biblical statements regarding homosexuality are pointed toward wanton sexual experiences outside of a monogamous, committed relationship.

This argument presupposes homosexual monogamous relationships did not exist during biblical times, or at least did not exist publicly. Evidence does not back this presupposition either; in antiquity, monogamous gay relationships existed openly.[38] Greco-Roman literature provides passages illustrating the beauty and compassion of same-sex love. Plato's *Symposium* (178C-180B) and Plutarch's *Dialogue on Love* (750B-751B and 752B-C) are but two examples.[39]

It is true Scripture does not explicitly mention monogamous homosexual relationships. But this lack of qualification does not undercut the force of the biblical prohibition. Rather, the lack of qualifications in scripture provides additional evidence the Biblical prohibitions on homosexual behavior are unconditional. Had Paul or the Levitical writer or Jesus for that matter wanted to set monogamous relationships as the paragon of intra-human fidelity, they could have said so explicitly. They didn't. We are called into covenant relationships with one another and our God, but those covenant relationships have boundaries and prohibitions. Having a monogamous relationship is not the ultimate point. The ultimate

---

[37] See James Brownson, *Bible Gender Sexuality: Reframing the Church's Debate on Same-Sex Relationships* (Grand Rapids: Eerdmans, 2013); Victor Furnish, *The Moral Teaching of Paul* (Nashville: Abingdon Press, 2009); Justin Lee, *Torn: Rescuing the Gospel from the Gays vs. Christians Debate* (Nashville: Jericho Books, 2013); Song, *Covenant and Calling;* Matthew Vines, *God and the Gay Christian: The Biblical Case in Support of Same-Sex Relationships* (New York: Convergent Books, 2015); and Ken Wilson, *A Letter to My Congregation* (Canton, MI: Read the Spirit Books, 2014).

[38] Gagnon, *The Bible and Homosexual Practice,* 350.

[39] Plato, "Symposium," in *Plato: Collected Dialogues,* edited by Edith Hamilton and Huntington Cairns (Princeton: Princeton UP, 1989), 533-534. Plutarch, "Dialogue on Love," *On Love, the Family and the Good Life: Selected Essays of Plutarch,* edited by Moses Hadas (Ann Arbor: University of Michigan, 1957), 307-308.

point is to have that covenant relationship with God's set criteria so that our faithfulness to another includes our faithfulness to God.

Robert Song argues that sex within a relationship gains meaning from the relationship surrounding it. Therefore, a committed and monogamous gay relationship in covenant and fidelity may provide a witness to God's fidelity and love resulting in a similar conclusion, though different form, to a committed and monogamous heterosexual marriage.[40] He argues the relationship defines the physical intimacy of the partners and not vice versa. The quality of the relationship matters more than the type of genital contact.

Utilizing Song's reasoning then, would not other types of marriage also warrant a divine seal of approval? If the criteria were only commitment and fidelity within the marriage, then couldn't incestuous marriage with the prerequisites of fidelity and covenant also witness to the glory of God? Would Song's standard also apply to polygamous marriages, so long as the members of those marriages remained in covenant with all other members of that marriage? Having established the validity of marriage as only commitment and fidelity within the marriage, Song is left with these logical conclusions. Song does not argue this; nor am I aware of other advocates of homosexual marriage arguing the merits of polygamy or incestuous unions. But the applicability of polygamy and incest as extensions of Song's thought undercut this argument.

So then what are the boundaries for covenant fidelity and marriage?

Marriage, according to Scripture, involves more than just commitment and fidelity within the marriage (Ephesians 5:22-33). A number of scholars argue that God sets forth a gender pattern for marriage in Genesis 1:27: *So God created humankind in his own image, in the image of God he created them; male and female he created them* [NRSV]. Marriage is a covenant in fidelity involving a male and a female. God purposefully created humanity in two gender types; those gender types are anatomically complementary. The rest of Scripture assumes this male/female pattern in marriage as this criterion appears in both the Old Testament and the New Testament (Hosea, Song of Songs, Ephesians 5 and Colossians 3.18-19). The Bible takes for

---

[40] Song, *Covenant and Calling*, 58.

granted that uniting in marriage occurs only between male and female genders.[41]

Jesus Himself assumes the male-female archetype in Mark 10:6-9: *[6] But from the beginning of creation 'God made them male and female.' [7] 'For this reason a man shall leave his father and mother and be joined to his wife, [8] and the two shall become one flesh.' So they are no longer two, but one flesh. [9] Therefore what God has joined together, let no one separate* [NRSV]. These verses occur within the larger context of a section on discipleship (8:22-10:52) within a passage on the lawfulness of divorce (10:1-12). The Pharisees asked Jesus to specify when divorce was lawful. While the questioners began with a Mosaic decree on divorce, Jesus moved the question from what made divorce permissible to what God intended for marriage. He quoted from Genesis 1:27, specifically the gendering of humanity, to declare marriage was only marriage when it involved one male and one female. Jesus continued with a quote from Genesis 2:24 detailing the beginning of marriage as the occasion when a man and woman come together as "one flesh." Jesus stands within the Jewish tradition's definition of marriage as one male and one female to the exclusion of all other definitions.

Genesis 1:27 and 2:24 provide a marriage gender pattern for Jewish and subsequent Christian enactment. The male and female gender differences allow for complement, fit and the sharing of resources between a husband and wife.[42] This match builds up both partners making the couple greater than the sum of its parts. The distinctions include anatomical and biological differences that allow for the possibility of procreation. The gender differences present in creation, per the Genesis passages, reflect the purpose and intent of the Creator.[43] Judaism and Christianity frame

---

[41] Brownson, *Bible Gender Sexuality*, 108.

[42] Terence Fretheim, "The Book of Genesis," *The New Interpreter's Bible*, Volume 1 (Nashville: Abingdon Press, 1994), 345. Additionally, this is not a book on complementarianism or egalitarianism within marriage. Other books can address those questions. If you come to this book looking to grind that axe, find another stone.

[43] Walter Brueggemann, *Genesis*, Interpretation Series (Atlanta: John Knox Press, 1982), 33.

marriage within the theology found in the creation narratives of ancient Israel. More than happenstance or tradition, the Bible posits marriage as exclusive to a man and a woman.

So is Marriage just for Making Babies?

In a word, NO. Victor Hamilton argues from the Genesis verses the ability to procreate is not the sole goal of marriage.[44] Obviously, procreation cannot happen without the involvement of a male and a female. However, per the Genesis accounts, marriage involves the forsaking of one family to create a new family—one without offspring at its inception. Becoming a new family entails more than a sexual experience with the potential for biological reproduction. The new couple now in covenant journey through life hand-in-hand as a unit. One flesh implies the man and the woman have taken on new self-understandings and a new unified identity.[45] This fundamentally shifts the prior perspectives of the man and the woman when each was single. The new husband and wife move from self-centered individual focus to a singular vantage point. This change in outlook and decision-making happens prior to, and includes the subsequent decision about, the conception of additional members of the family.

Jesus' words in Mark 10 allude to an anatomical complementarity within the purpose of creation for marriage.[46] The Creator's design included a gender fit; Jesus builds his response to his questioners on this understanding. God fashioned the masculine and feminine genders for his glory and for the benefit of one another in marriage. God created humans as male and female with the intention of uniting physically, emotionally, and spiritually in marriage

---

[44] Victor P. Hamilton, *The Book of Genesis: Chapters 1-17*, NICOT (Grand Rapids: Eerdmans 1990), 181.

[45] Fretheim, "The Book of Genesis," 354.

[46] Sharyn Dowd, *Reading Mark: A Literary and Theological Commentary on the Second Gospel*, Reading the New Testament, Vol. 2 (Macon, GA: Smyth & Helwys Publishing, 2000), 102; and Larry W. Hurtado, *Mark*, Understanding the Bible Commentary Series, Book 2 (Ada, MI: Baker Books, 1989), 161.

A point of clarification is necessary. I do not use gender and sexuality as synonyms. Gender signifies cultural and societal characteristics as well as roles of the masculine and feminine categories. Sexuality refers to anatomical and biological differences between males and females.

This gendered union in marriage includes a complementarity that allows for procreation, but does not necessitate procreation. The distinct anatomy and biology of males and females provides the means for a wife and husband in marriage to follow Genesis 1:28: *God blessed them, and God said to them, "Be fruitful and multiply, fill the earth and subdue it; and have dominion over the fish of the sea and over the birds of the air and over every living thing that moves upon the earth."* Procreation is a blessing; the ability to have children is a gift. Procreation is not a command. Nor is procreation a necessary essential to marriage. The reality is some married couples are infertile; some choose to *increase in number* through adoption; and some choose to remain childless. The lack of children through procreation does not invalidate a marriage anymore than the birth of a child out of wedlock elevates the sexual union of that child's non-married biological parents into a matrimonial state. Marriage does not hang upon the production of offspring; the production of offspring does not make a relationship a marriage. The point is gender distinction allows for the possibility of procreation; it does not necessitate it.

At the risk of having overstated the distinction, let me emphasize that marriage and procreation are connected within God's framework. Procreation is not to occur outside of marriage. God may will a marriage without procreation; God does not will procreation outside of marriage [aside from the Incarnation of Jesus Christ!].

Is Homosexual behavior prohibited because that activity is infertile?

Song argues the church should affirm gay relationships since marriage is not inherently for procreation, removing this as a barrier to the affirmation of homosexual marriage within the church.[47] Husbands and wives know full well that intercourse provides a physical closeness beyond the creation of offspring. Sex within the bond of marriage is for God's glory

---

[47] Song, *Covenant and Calling*, xi.

primarily, making the production of offspring a secondary good.[48] The argument the Bible rejects homosexual relationships because of an inability to yield offspring is specious. The scriptural rejection of homosexual behavior has no basis in the inability of gay partners to procreate.[49]

Paul is typically cast as maintaining procreation is necessary to marriage; however, upon deeper examination, this argument crumbles. Paul's rejection of homosexual behavior, inclusive of gay marriage, has nothing to do with a lack of procreativity. Paul's rejection of homosexual behavior is not based solely or primarily upon horizontal relationships, inclusive of the production of offspring, but upon the vertical relationship of the gay person to God.[50] Homosexual practice is immoral and offensive to God. Scripture does not qualify this prohibition in either the Old Testament or New Testament as having a basis in the non-procreative potential of gay partners. The prohibition is based, per the biblical warrant, upon offending God through sinful transgression (Leviticus 11:45).

The Bible prohibits homosexual behavior. Jesus Christ builds upon the Genesis creation accounts by stating that marriage is between a man and woman. Some scholars who theologically affirm both homosexual behavior and gay marriages acknowledge their view is contrary to the scriptural mandate.[51] With very rare exceptions, biblical scholars recognize that the Bible prohibits homosexual behavior. The scriptural witness is

---

[48] Paul Evdokimov, "The Sacrament of Love: The Nuptial Mystery in the Light of Orthodox Tradition," *Theology and Sexuality: Classic and Contemporary Readings*, ed. Eugene Rogers (Malden, MA: Blackwell Publishers, 2002), 188.

[49] Sprinkle, *People to Be Loved*, 67. God intends procreation to occur within marriage. Procreation and marriage are not therefore completely separated. Genesis 2:24 speaks of a husband and wife becoming "one flesh." This speaks to their union as a couple in becoming a new family as well as the potential for the production of a child made from the DNA of the husband and wife.

[50] Gagnon, *The Bible and Homosexual Practice*, 337.

[51] See Song, *Covenant and Calling*; Luke Timothy Johnson, "Disputed Questions: Debate and Discernment, Scripture and Spirit," and William Loader, *Two Views on Homosexuality, the Bible and the Church*, ed. Preston Sprinkle, Counterpoints Bible & Theology Series (Grand Rapids Zondervan, 2016).

clear and without qualification. Scripture makes no allowance for homosexual behavior just as it makes no allowance for heterosexual behavior outside of marriage.[52]

Is a Life without Sex Worth Living?

Our culture would say no. We are animals and as animals we just want to hump. The bible says something else; and deep down we know there is more to life. The orgasm is not the apex of human existence or expression. While sex is pleasurable, life has deeper gifts to offer.

The biblical mandate for gay persons is no different than the scriptural command for single heterosexual believers as it comes to sexual behavior—live a chaste and celibate life (Romans 13:13 and Ephesians 5:3). Matthew Vines, a gay believer who affirms gay marriage, asserts celibacy is a specific call from God as opposed to a biblical imposition.[53] In his reasoning, individual believers who are gay must receive a personal directive from God to live celibate lives. The church therefore cannot impress celibacy upon believers as a category based upon sexual orientation. Celibacy denies gay persons the inherent good of marriage, i.e. living in covenant and fidelity. Gay believers therefore may choose to live a celibate life; however, celibacy is not a default status for gay persons. Marriage inclusive of sexual intimacy within that covenant relationship is an option for gay persons who have not received a specific directive from God to live a celibate life, per Vines.

Vines' point that celibacy only applies to those who receive a specific and personal call misses the mark. He concedes that homosexual behavior

---

[52] Welcoming and affirming proponents may level the charge that evangelical churches widespread acceptance of divorce and second marriages undercuts their stance against homosexual behavior. They would have justification in doing so. Jesus alludes to homosexual prohibition in Mark 10 while speaking directly against divorce and second (or third or fourth or…) marriages. And yet, most evangelical churches accept heterosexual divorce and additional marriages as an accommodation to the culture despite the biblical witness against both. For consistency in biblical interpretation, theology and practice, evangelicals need to address divorce and re-marriages.

[53] Vines, *God and the Gay Christian*, 44.

is legitimate only within gay marriage; while he does not follow the biblical mandate in prohibiting homosexual activity, he does affirm appropriate homosexual behavior occurs only within a committed monogamous relationship.[54] Ostensibly, he would agree unmarried believers are to remain celibate, whether heterosexual or homosexual. He agrees sexual purity is a command of each and every follower of Christ, without each and every believer receiving a specific call to live a chaste and celibate life until marriage. Celibacy before marriage is presupposed by scripture. Believers in Jesus are all called to a celibate lifestyle until marriage. Vines wishes to include gay marriage as acceptable to God; however, as has been shown above, godly marriage is between a man and a woman only per scripture. The call to celibacy then applies to gay persons as well as it applies to unmarried heterosexuals. Celibacy is part of the cost of discipleship for single believers, whether gay or heterosexual.

Another argument against celibacy says since creation is inherently good and sexuality is part of the created order, then sexual intimacy must be inherently good; so then, if sexual intimacy is inherently good, a denial of that intimacy harms creation.[55] This is faulty theology as it subordinates the doctrine of redemption to the doctrine of creation, which happens a lot [as shown in Chapter Three!]. Genesis 1 does witness to the goodness of creation. God made creation and it is GOOD. But two chapters later, the Bible witnesses to human sinfulness through the disobedience of Adam and Eve. The inherent good of creation was masked by sin and rebellion against God after the Fall. Sin affects all aspects of creation, and therefore necessitates the need for redemption of all creation. Through redemption in Christ, God reconciles humanity and creation to himself (Romans 3:24 and Ephesians 1:7). Only through redemption can humanity and the world become what the Creator intended at creation; see Revelation 21:5. Only through a relationship with Jesus Christ can we subordinate our stubborn willfulness to His majesty. Simply having certain anatomical parts does not imply anything we do with those same certain anatomical parts exhibits the goodness of creation. We need redemption. All of us. ALL OF US.

---

[54] Ibid., 137.

[55] Ibid., 45-46.

Didn't Christianity do this with slavery and women in ministry centuries ago?

A word about *progressive revelation* seems in order. Progressive revelation refers to the belief that through history, God reveals Truth and Purpose. Over time, more and more of this revelation takes place. The Jews of the Exodus worshipped YHWH through sacrifices and the Law. The early church worshipped Jesus Christ through faith, hope and love. And believers continue to progress in obedience and worship. Progressive revelation says that God's unveiling is incomplete and continues. What was once believed as divine truth can be viewed as outdated as we learn and come to God in a greater way. What we know in the moment about God and following God is not fixed but open to future correction. That's *progressive revelation.*

Those who affirm homosexual behavior often parallel this issue with the Church's past stances on slavery and women in ministry. In linking these three issues, those proponents hope to show that the Church's past change in its understanding of slavery and women in ministry opens the door to a reconsideration of the biblical warrant against homosexual behavior.

Per the Great Commandment in Matthew 19:19 and the lack of biblical endorsement, churches today disavow slavery in its many insidious forms. However, during the colonial period of the United States and during the European colonization of Africa and the Americas, Scripture was used to justify slavery. Slavery proponents took passages out of context and misinterpreted them to posit slavery as an institution with scriptural backing.[56] Those with a hermeneutic of progressive revelation argue just as Christians for a time misunderstood biblical passages on slavery, so too Christians now misunderstand passages on homosexual behavior.

This is an invalid comparison that does not make the argument supporters of homosexual behavior intend.[57] The Church did at times use Scripture to justify slavery; the Church owns this sin. It was wrong then

---

[56] Verses that appear to tolerate slavery include Leviticus 25:44, Ephesians 6:5-11 and Colossians 3:22-4:1.

[57] Gagnon and Dan Via, *Homosexuality and the Bible*, 45.

and ungodly. In my opinion, those who knowingly promoted the slave economy through specific preaching, rewriting the Bible and espousing dastardly theology now enjoy the bitter fruits of Hell rather than the sweet bliss of Heaven. That grievous episode of promoting slavey doesn't equate to God calling followers to sexual holiness.

Pro-slavery arguments from Scripture could at best find verses tolerant of the practice; there are not verses that explicitly promote and advocate for slavery. By contrast, there are any number of biblical verses that witness to physical and spiritual freedom in Jesus Christ as well as the equality of all human beings before the throne of God, both as sinners and as potentially redeemed believers (a few: Romans 8:20-21, 2 Corinthians 3:17, Galatians 5:1 and 13 and 1 Peter 2:16).

Regarding homosexual behavior, in contrast, the Bible contains explicit passages in the Old and New Testaments and Jesus' own words regarding the gendered purpose of marriage that both prohibit homosexual practice and promote monogamy between a man and woman. A progressive revelation seeking to justify homosexual behavior would have to deny outright specific passages of the Bible. Pro-slavery advocates relied upon scriptural tolerance; pro-homosexual behavior does not even have this thin ledge upon which to stand.

Others seek to make a link between the evolution of the church's views on women in ministry and the affirmation of homosexual behavior. In both the Old and New Testaments, God often placed women in positions of leadership and in most cases did so against the prevailing cultural view of women at those times.[58] Despite this, the church has not had universal affirmation of women in ministry. The disputed interpretations of 1 Corinthians 14:33-35 and 1 Timothy 2:11-15 provide the primary sources for ecclesial disagreement on the role of women in the church. Even taking these passages into account—and interpreting them as universally valid rather than as contextually specific—the weight of Scripture is toward gender equality, not against it (Galatians 3:28). There are positive examples of women in leadership in both testaments. Paul lists 10 women of note,

[58] These include Numbers 27:1-11, Judges 4:4-5, Esther 4:15-17, Luke 8.1-3, 10:38-42, John 4:1-26, Acts 1:12-14, 18:24-26, 21:7-9 and Romans 16:1-3.

including Deacon Phoebe in Romans 16:1 [Yes *Deacon.* The Greek word in Romans is *diakonos*, which means Deacon.].

There is not a parallel between women in ministry and affirming homosexual behavior since there are no affirmations of homosexual behavior in either testament and there exist specific prohibitions against homosexual behavior in both. [59] Regarding women in ministry, a progressive reading on these issues arises from within Scripture, not outside of it, given the frequency of women placed in ministry in the Bible. The same cannot be said for justifying homosexual behavior. Any progressive revelation supporting gay marriage must come from outside the biblical warrant, in explicit contradiction to the biblical warrant itself. An analogy between supporting women in ministry and affirming homosexual practice is therefore untenable. Within the Christian tradition and Scripture, arguments against slavery and for women in ministry do not lend support to an argument affirming homosexual practice.

Is this issue really about the Bible?

There are a lot of issues upon which Christians can agreeably disagree. This issue makes it more difficult because the greater issue is not homosexual behavior but one's view of the Bible. The acceptance or denial of homosexual behavior as godly unavoidably represents a faith community's view of Scripture. [60] Churches that affirm homosexual behavior must rely upon a biblical hermeneutic of progressive revelation. Experience in this reading methodology corrects the biblical material as intellectual and societal findings offer alternatives to the imperatives of Scripture. [61] The biblical revelation yields its authority to human sensibilities and attitudes based on the surrounding secular culture forcing

---

[59] For more on analogizing and the progressive revelation hermeneutic see William J. Webb, *Slaves, Women & Homosexuals: Exploring the Hermeneutics of Cultural Analysis* (Downers Grove: IVP Books, 2001).

[60] Stanley Grenz, *Welcoming but Not Affirming* (Louisville: Westminster John Knox Press, 1998), 89. Matthew Vines disagrees vehemently. He argues that one can affirm the authority of Scripture and support homosexual behavior (2).

[61] Schmidt, *Straight & Narrow?*, 58.

churches to choose which verses to leave out of their Bible studies and preaching. This hermeneutic diminishes the Bible's ability to confront and challenge believers. Instead of informing a congregation's theology and practice, the Bible becomes a document after the fact supporting what a congregation believes and does. This hermeneutic lacks consistency, evidence, and does not fit within the Jewish or Christian understanding of canon. It does not fit within an evangelical understanding of the Bible as set forth earlier in this chapter.[62]

What has Christianity said about Homosexuality since the Bible?

Josephus was one of the earliest Christian-era writers to denounce homosexual behavior.[63] He was not a believer; he was a Jew who wrote a Jewish history for Roman readers. Josephus wrote that homosexual behavior and gay relationships defiled the gendered complementarity laid

---

[62] Some would argue that our twenty-first century understandings of the universe, psychology, anthropology, etc. contradict the biblical witness so that as we learn more about homosexuality—and sexuality in general—Bible readers should expect to disregard verses that contradict human knowledge. Isn't this what the church has done with verses that allude to a three-story universe or a cosmology that assumes a seven-day creation? What then hinders the employment of a similar hermeneutic with regard to prohibitions of homosexual behavior? This is not an apples to apples analogy. There are profound differences between accepting literal interpretations that contradict archaeological and cosmological findings and taking scriptural prohibitions against homosexual practice at face value. The Bible does not present itself as a history book or a book about the inner workings of the universe. Rather, the Bible presents itself as book telling the story of God and how God's story impacts the story of every living person. Belief in God's story does not depend upon one's cosmology; it does depend upon one's relationship to God through grace and obedience. The message of grace and the call to obedience come through the biblical witness of Jesus Christ, inclusive of biblical commands concerning personal conduct. This includes prohibitions against homosexual behavior.

[63] William Loader, *Making Sense of Sex: Attitudes towards Sexuality in Early Jewish and Christian Literature* (Grand Rapids Eerdmans, 2013), 135. Josephus, *Against Apion Book II.*

out in Genesis 1 & 2.[64] The Alexandrian author Philo, who was also Jewish, wrote that homosexual behavior contradicts appropriate living.[65] He used much of the same reasoning as Josephus. The Christians Patristic writers of the first several centuries continued this line of reasoning that prohibited homosexual practice.[66] For the most part, this instantiated both the prevailing biblical interpretation against homosexual behavior and Christian tradition thereafter.

From the lengthy argument above a reader may ask if the Word is welcoming. God's prohibition on homosexual behavior accounts for a minute portion of the scriptural witness. We aren't to dismiss those few verses obviously. The Gospel is a Welcoming Word because it points us to Jesus Christ. It directs us to the foot of the cross where we may lay down all of our sins whatever they may be, and we all have lots and lots. It invites us to an empty tomb to see a Risen Savior and know we are not so broken the Great Physician can't fix us, not so far gone that the Shepherd can't find us and not so misshapen the Potter can't remake us. This is a welcome message no matter who you are. You are loved by a gracious God. You are called to relationship with the Son of God. You are welcomed to the journey of faith led by the Holy Spirit. It is a Welcoming Word!

The next chapter will share how we the Church can exhibit that welcome.

---

[64] Furnish, *The Moral Teaching of Paul,* 67.

[65] Loader, The *New Testament on Sexuality*, 33. Philo, *Volume VII.*

[66] Grenz, *Welcoming but Not Affirming,* 64. Justin Martyr, *First Apology 27*; Cyprian of Carthage, *Letters 1:8*; Eusebius of Caesarea, *Proof of the Gospel 4:10*; John Chrysostom, *Homilies on Titus 5, Homilies on Matthew 3:3, Homilies on Romans 4.*

Study Questions

1. What is your view of scripture? What is your church's view of scripture? How does this view affect your understanding of homosexuality?
2. Using the material in Appendix A, how do you react to the six verses that reference homosexuality in the Bible?
3. Why are God-imposed boundaries important in our growing discipleship?
4. What are heterosexual boundaries God has imposed for growing in discipleship?
5. What are non-sexual boundaries God has imposed for growing in discipleship?
6. Do these boundaries receive as much attention as homosexual boundaries in your church? If not, why?
7. Pray God would convict you of your sin. Commit to confess that sin, repent and know grace fully. Trust Jesus relieves you of guilt and shame by His Blood.

Chapter Five

The Welcoming Community

People need connection. People want connection. God made us so we would, through Jesus Christ, connect to Him. God made us so we would connect to one another through His love for us. We do this most naturally as brothers and sisters of faith, through the Church. It is a spiritual need. It is a social need.

I believe that God desires for Christians to invite non-believers into these connections to meet these needs. All people need these connections. Our churches have ignored these connective needs for most groups except married couples and families. We leave singles out. We leave widows and widowers out. We leave gay persons out. For all of our bible-thumping, we fail to take seriously Paul's words in 1 Corinthians 7 regarding his preference for singleness over marriage. I write this as one married. I also write this as one who has sought to foster welcome for singles in church.

We had a lot of twenty-somethings at the church in Texas I served. A few older members took charge in creating safe space for these young people. Some had finished college and weren't sure what was next. Some had started careers. Some worked but lacked specific direction. Some were engaged. Some were single. Some were gay. They all needed community; they all needed a church to love them. This group offered community in the name of Jesus Christ.

This group soon became the biggest one in the church. They served. They participated. They grew in their relationships with Jesus. The leaders maintained safe space for honest and frank discussions. The dear souls in this group provided the same for one another. They lived life together. They were known by God and they knew God. They were known by one another and they knew one another.

I had some discussion with the leaders of this group about the church purchasing a house to provide a place for deep faith community to further develop. The house would provide space for people to live life together more closely and intimately. Functioning as a household, cooking together, eating together, relying upon one another in momentary life stresses and celebrating communally—things taken for granted by married couples. For singles, these opportunities seem unreachable. The Bible's admonition against same-sex intimacy is not an admonition against physical, emotional, and spiritual intimacy. We wanted to provide space for those singles to build core relationships. We wanted the church to provide an actual alternative to loneliness, to provide ways to meet the spiritual and social need for connection.

We did not pull the trigger, sadly. Our leaders became house families at a local university, providing similar community albeit it to dorm students. I have some regrets about not pushing this forward. It was biblical and it would have stood as a witness to what Jesus offers while providing a strong contrast to a wholly negative message of forsaken intimacy that gay persons typically hear when Jesus comes up. Intentional communities are one way a church can provide a place for gay persons to flourish, find support, accountability and serve others through their faith.

Wesley Hill has served Christendom through his work *Spiritual Friendship*.[67] Friendship is a voluntary yoking of one person to another. In many ways, friendship has as many implied commitments as explicitly committed relationships. Hill makes a contrast between companionship, which is more by association, and true friendship, which involves chosen allegiance.

The Church is to be a place for deep friendships among faith family. Our churches exhibit this in many ways through Deacon bodies, Sunday School classes and so forth. We have a Sunday morning bible study class that has been together for decades. They know one another deeply, having walked through the ups and downs of life together. They are family to one another. Their friendship transcends human bonds; it has taken on a form

---

[67] Hill, *Spiritual Friendship: Finding Love in the Church as a Celibate Gay Christian* (Grand Rapids: Brazos Press, 2015).

of faithfulness to Christ. The Church can offer space and opportunities to form deep friendships, connecting people through God's love of us and His command for us to love one another.

Our men's ministry is an example. We seek to connect men into small groups of 4-6 to meet regularly, know one another, and grow in relationship. Over time, these men grow close. They rely upon one another in hard times; they celebrate with one another in jubilant times.

Each of us needs the intimacy of deep friendships. Each of us. The Church can foster this intentionally with singles and gay persons serving as exemplars of this. There are trials singles and gay persons go through that married couples do not. Those unique trials offer opportunities for God's presence in a new personal way. The greater Church can learn from this.

There are other myriad ways to offer community. Each takes investment and commitment from the church. Each takes intention. Each takes a willingness to embrace. God calls us to nothing less.

Many evangelical churches, while holding clear understandings of Scripture and its redemptive Gospel message, have failed to account for hospitality, as either a theological necessity or a Christian practice. Rather than welcoming gay persons into a place where they might hear the message of Jesus and His offer of liberation from the chains of this world, many have demonized and ostracized these souls. Instead of preaching a gospel of love and a message of grace, clergy have cast derision and exclusion. Rather than witnessing a posture of open arms, gay persons have encountered clenched fists from those who profess to represent Jesus Christ.

Some questions this chapter will answer: what is welcome? What are aspects of congregational hospitality and care for others? How does the church appropriately welcome the stranger into its midst? From where does this impetus arise and how is it sustained within a defined community of faith? How does the hospitable community remain a community as it welcomes new people into that community?

I have had the privilege to receive congregational hospitality and to witness welcome. My wife and I were newlyweds having relocated from the familiar confines of the Southeast to New Jersey to start seminary. We very much felt like outsiders in that environment. Attending seminary meant our brains worked hard. We wanted a church home that would work and feed our souls. We wanted that church family. We visited a Baptist church in the area. The service was fine. The people seemed pleasant. No one greeted us. No one introduced themselves. No one asked us our names. We tried another with a similar result. We were, in all honestly, becoming discouraged and brought up the idea of just going to the Sunday chapel service at the University. We tried one more church upon the recommendation of a friend. The church was located in the middle of Trenton, known more for its poverty and crime than it's illustrious industrial history.

We got up early one Sunday morning and without directions—this was pre-smart phone and map apps—we drove around the city. For 45 minutes we drove around the city looking for this church [it's a fair question to ask why we didn't get directions from our friend and I don't have a good answer for you]. We were 5 minutes from the appointed start time of worship and about to throw in the towel when we turned a corner at Centre St. and found the church.

It was a big building but a small church. It had a magnificent sanctuary but only a handful of people. Upon entering, an older person said hello. After church, we were invited to fellowship where someone put a plate in front of me with a small piece of cake [it may not be the healthiest post-worship snack but it was welcoming]. We got to talk with members and the pastor as everyone sat down with some refreshments. They opened their arms to my wife and I. Even though we had some twang in our accents and came from other parts, they offered us hospitality. And we returned the next Sunday and the next…

Welcoming others is at the core of what it means to follow Jesus Christ (Acts 2:44-45). [68] Hospitality means welcoming someone into your presence or your community. That someone offers nothing tangible to the host; hospitality stands in stark contrast to a *quid pro quo* relationship. The host offers welcome simply for the sake of offering it, expecting nothing in return. Hospitality derives from genuine interest in that person. It means

---

[68] Amy G Oden, *God's Welcome: Hospitality for a Gospel-Hungry World* (Cleveland: Pilgrim Press, 2008), 11.

responding to that person's presence with enthusiasm and greeting. Jesus welcomed any who would hear him. The religious leaders of his day considered many of those welcomed by our Lord to be outcasts, sinners beyond reach and defiled people.[69] Jesus responded to these people of the margins with compassion, love and attention. As imitators of Jesus, Christians are to live lives of hospitality toward others.

Welcome comprises more of an attitude and orientation than a mechanism or list of prescribed actions.[70] It is a way of being, not a set of rehearsed motions. Hospitality begins with an intention, a disposition and an attitude; then, hospitality flows outward to others through physical acts. Having received the welcome of God through Jesus, believers become purveyors of hospitality to others.

Hospitality originates with God; believers are recipients. Welcoming witnesses to the salvation of the host—having received God's hospitality as an unearned gift. Welcoming witnesses and seeks to mimic the ultimate host, Jesus himself, who relieved visitors, strangers and outsiders of the burden of their sins through his open arms. The hospitality from God then is redirected toward others--strangers, non-believers, and those known—from an overflow of joy, assurance and peace (Hebrews 13:2). Welcome is a physical and tangible testimony of the Gospel arising from God's Spirit of grace and mercy.[71]

The early church considered hospitality as one of its chief attributes and missional tools. In its first few centuries, pagans and non-believers knew of Christianity through the welcome of Christians. This hospitality toward others contributed to the rise of the church in the Roman Empire. The early church patriarch Tertullian offers several quotes that illustrate the force of hospitality: "To no less a post than this has God called them, and they dare not try to evade it. We have filled up every place belonging to you—islands,

---

[69] Ibid., 35-37. There are other typological stories of welcome found in Scripture. These include Joshua 2 and 6, Ruth, 1 Kings 17:7-24, Matthew 4:18-22, Matthew 22:1-14, Matthew 25:31-46, Luke 5:1-11, Luke 14:1-14, and John 4:1-26.

[70] Amy G. Oden, *And You Welcomed Me: A Sourcebook on Hospitality in Early Christianity* (Nashville: Abingdon Press, 2001), 14.

[71] Oden, *God's Welcome*, 15.

castles, caves, prisons, palace, city forum. We leave you your temples only."[72] And again: "It is our care of the helpless, our practice of loving kindness that brands us in the eyes of many of our opponents. 'Only look,' they say, 'look how they love one another!'"[73]

This openness to relationships with strangers and the non-utilization of people presented a new dynamic of grace and mercy to the first-century Mediterranean world through welcome. The early church offered hospitality to non-believers in a manner that was non-threatening and inviting.[74] The Church clearly took stances against many cultural practices including infanticide, the treatment of the poor and the economic stratification of the society; these positions ran counter to the culture and against the status quo. But the early Church welcomed each person who wanted to encounter the Risen Jesus, no exceptions.

Welcome as a spiritual practice has its origin in the worship of God. As one welcomes, greets, and provides care to another, that host honors God. The Christian host acknowledges the *imago dei* within each human being so the host serves God through serving others.[75] Hospitable believers offer praise and adoration to God through the care of strangers. Love towards the stranger is love of God. The Reformers utilized this theological link between hospitality and recognition of the Creator within his creatures.[76]

While hospitality treats others as ends in themselves, it also encapsulates promise and hope. Christians do not offer welcome and love to strangers to get them to join the church or the community. They offer hospitality to introduce the recipient into a relationship with God.[77] Hospitality comes from God to humanity and seeks to return humanity to God.

---

[72] Tertullian, "Apology," *Ante-Nicene Fathers*, Vol. 3 (Peabody, MA: Hendrickson Publishers, 1994), 45.

[73] Ibid., 46.

[74] Christine D. Pohl, *Making Room: Recovering Hospitality as a Christian Tradition* (Grand Rapids Eerdmans, 1999), 69.

[75] Pseudo-Clementine, "Recognitions of Clement," *Ante-Nicene Fathers*, Vol. 8 (Peabody, MA: Hendrickson Publishers, 1994), 148-149.

[76] Pohl, *Making Room*, 63.

[77] Oden, *God's Welcome*, 12.

Our contemporary culture is one of "stranger-danger" and suspicion towards people we do not know. This brings forward a consideration of the costs of welcome. Opening oneself to a stranger, inviting that person close, has inherent risk.[78] It is dangerous. Hospitality exposes the host. When you stand with arms wide open, you are vulnerable. This vulnerability extends beyond physical peril—the host risks receiving the very sentiment that hospitality is designed to combat: rejection. Others may well spurn Christian welcome. The open arms of embrace leave followers of Jesus exposed and vulnerable.

Jesus Christ embodies both the host and guest (Luke 24:13-35).[79] Jesus welcomes, and is the one welcomed. Jesus makes space for others and is the one for whom we make space. He stands as the ultimate example of rejection, bearing the rejection of God and humanity on the cross. He also stands as the ultimate example of hospitality given humanity's rejection of him does not have the final word. The cross provides the bridge so humans "are no longer foreigners and strangers" (Ephesians 2:19). The resurrection offers us reconciliation; it provides the means and purpose for our offering hospitality. As we offer hospitality, God brings us closer to himself. Our dependence upon God increases. With arms wide open, exposed and assailable, hosts rely upon God for protection.[80] We witness God at work through our vulnerability (2 Corinthians 12:9).

Another dynamic of welcome involves making space for the other. This gets to underlying contradictions within hospitality. It provides space to strangers, who by definition are dislocated and without proper space. Welcome can be thought of as a miniature reconciliation drama: as Jesus reconciles us to God, the Church reconciles outsiders to fellowship with Jesus. This ongoing action profoundly impacts the host (be it an individual or for the purposes of this project a community) from which the hospitality arises. As others are welcomed into the community, hosts must allow space for those welcomed. The community changes as it encounters new people.

---

[77] Pohl, *Making Room*, 94

[78] Ibid., 17.

[79] Jean Vanier, *Encountering the Other* (New York: Paulist Press, 2006), 54.

As seats are offered to strangers at the table by the host, the table expands, seats are added, and so forth. The community invariably shifts. Oden terms this de-centering.[81] De-centering allows the community to offer grace and truth. It also enables the community to receive wounded strangers into its midst.

This dynamic has the potential to, and frankly likelihood of, creating conflict within the community.[82] Adding new elements creates unease. As the table expands and new people are added to the community, this forces a reorientation of previous members. A simple illustration: I've had many opportunities to witness worship guests sit in places which are typically occupied by regular members. Those regulars come upon their usual spot and see new people sitting there. While it may seem like just a seat, that regular position affords fellowship and connection to regulars with longstanding placement nearby. It affords familiarity. When broken, unknowingly by visitors, it can cause harm. I've thankfully never witnessed a regular ask a guest to move. I've seen many a stern look, and I've heard a few comments. This is de-centering on a micro level. But God works in this de-centering.

To this point, it may sound as though de-centering obligates only the host. Not so. The hospitality offered welcomes strangers into a defined and distinct community. Hospitality invites the welcomed into a relationship with another entity that has content and identity, commitments and pre-existing relationships.[83] While the community makes space for recipients of the welcome, it does not lose the marks that formed and bound the community in the first place. The welcomed, through hospitality, enter the space of the community as well as its traditions, language, and values. There is an obligation upon the welcomed to move toward the community even as the community offers hospitality and open arms to the welcomed.[84] The hospitable community is a place offering far more than mere indulgence and comfort. It offers insight, change and transformation.

---

[81] Oden, *And You Welcomed Me*, 15.

[82] Ibid., 29-30.

[83] Pohl, *Making Room*, 83.

[84] Jean Vanier, *Community and Growth* (New York: Paulist Press, 1989), 77.

The change does not come from the community per se, either as a demand or catalyst. The community is simply the conduit through which the new member, who has received welcome and hospitality, encounters God (Hebrews 10:24-25). The community simply communicates the message of Christ's welcome to the stranger, offering a witness of the love of Jesus to the outsider. The community provides social hospitality but only as a means to direct the welcomed into divine hospitality through a relationship with Jesus Christ.

The community through its hospitality invites the welcomed to belong. Belonging is not an end in itself. It is a welcome in order to become. Hospitality offers the stranger an opportunity to become more. It welcomes the stranger into a safe space to grow and receive transformation.[85] It also beckons the welcomed to leave their own space—their understandings, identity and worldview—and enter into the culture of a hospitable community.

Christian hospitality that offers a welcome devoid of transformation is not true hospitality, as in the case of same-sex behavior affirming churches. Community within the Christian tradition does not exist as an end in itself.[86] Community for the sake of community is idolatrous and false. Christian community has as its origination and purpose the love of God. God's love provides the foundation and impetus for community. Glorifying God is the goal and end of this community. Only God provides healing; only God provides redemption and true growth; only God does this. Community is therefore a means toward reconciliation, both on vertical and horizontal planes. Community builds connections between people. More importantly, community provides a connection between people and God.

One critique of *welcoming and affirming* churches is the lack of purpose in moving gay persons toward transformation and healing. The Gospel is not *come as you are and stay that way*; the Gospel is instead *repent for the Kingdom of God is at hand.* This is a redemptive, salvific message all need to hear. The tacit message of these churches seems to be gay persons do not need transformation. Affirming behavior endorses it. So then, is it

---

[85] Vanier, *From Brokenness to Community*, 10.

[86] Ibid., 49.

possible for these churches to truly preach a message of redemption and change?

Christian community offers hospitality, welcome and much more. It invites strangers to come as they are in order to receive and be made new (2 Corinthians 5:17). That reception, as an outgrowth of accepting a welcome, is to grow into the people God intended, just as the hosts seek to do within that community. God binds people together through community and that community comes by way of hospitality. As Parker Palmer writes: "Community is finally a religious phenomenon. There is nothing capable of binding together willful, broken human selves except some transcendent power."[87]

Read this closely. Change is not a condition for entrance into the Christian community. It is a later expectation, yes. It is not a condition for being welcomed. There is not a prior condition to hearing Jesus, not a behavioral cover charge, not an entrance exam. Jesus did not direct His followers to say the following: *If you change, then you are welcome to join me in my community. Conform and belong. Agree with us and we will embrace you. To be with us, you must be like us.*

That's not what the Church does. We welcome others to Christ through His Body. Individual abilities, talent and God's direction impact the church community. The church definitely impacts and affects the new members without a doubt but relationships are bi-directional. A church is made up of many Christ following people. Same Jesus, different people—making for an organic and growing community of believers.

The hospitable church proclaims a message of a "welcoming and mutually transforming" relationship with God and one another.[88] The transformation is not one-sided; it affects the welcomed and the welcomers. The goal of the community is to become like Jesus Christ as opposed to members merging into some homogenous mass. Rather than having outsiders strive to be like insiders, the Christian community invites non-

---

[87] Vanier, *Community and Growth*, 44, quotation from Parker J. Palmer, *A Place Called Community* (Pendle Hill Publishing, Philadelphia, 1977), 18.

[88] Hirsch, *Redeeming Sex,* 196.

believers to seek after God as the community members themselves seek after God.

Christian welcome is part and parcel of the Christian faith (Acts 2:46). It embodies the worship of God. Hospitality involves exposing oneself and one's community to welcome the stranger. This openness also opens the community to new relationships. These new relationships shift the community but do not untie it from its distinctive moorings. Hospitality pushes the hospitable community to enlarge its space to potentially incorporate the welcomed into its midst. [89] The path toward this incorporation, the simultaneous enlarging and maintaining of boundaries is complicated and not without difficulty.[90] The welcomed are not simply welcomed to a vacuous space or into an amorphous entity. The welcomed through hospitality are welcomed to *something*. Acknowledging difference and distinction, definitions and identities does not negate or nullify hospitality; it offers a deeper platform from which relationships arise.[91] A community secure in its identity and mission will navigate these difficult spots. This navigation will rely in large part upon those essential practices within the community that help define it.

Going back to my wife and I finding a church in Trenton, NJ, they got to know us. We got to know them. Over time we learned names and roles at the church. We learned about their illustrious history and past leadership. They learned of our southern roots, family backgrounds, and hopes for the future. We did not threaten them. They did not scare us. But initially we both made ourselves vulnerable to this encounter. Over time, that church community blessed our journey and growth as Jesus followers. We enhanced theirs. This is de-centering. It is part and parcel to welcoming others to the Gospel.

The success or failure of the navigation of hospitality for a community may well rest upon an understanding of covenant.[92] The community relies upon God the Father, Son, and Holy Spirit for its vision, values and mission

---

[89] Pohl, *Making Room,* 39.

[90] Ibid., 127.

[91] Ibid., 135.

[92] Ibid., 136.

(Romans 12:1-2). Within this identity is the command to go forth loving God and others (Mark 12:29-31). From the perspective of the welcoming community, hospitality is both a reliance upon and a following of God. Through implication, this covenant extends beyond Lord and servant. It branches out to extend hospitality, and covenant love to non-believers, strangers and those outside the covenant community. In this way, hospitality becomes pro-active, rather than exhibiting a reactive dynamic. The welcome is extended to bring others into covenant. The welcome of the community implies an offer for the stranger to enter and be changed through the transformative power of our Lord and Savior Jesus Christ. Hospitality offers reconciliation through the offer of belonging, which is an offer to become in like manner to those already part of the hospitable community.

Elizabeth Newman in *Untamed Hospitality* offers a theologically sound and biblically based understanding of what it means for a community of faith to welcome others into its midst. She laments the current theological understanding of what Christian hospitality is and is not. Whereas secular incarnations of hospitality focus upon self-actualization, entertainment and catering to the perceived needs of individual customers, God calls the church to offer something far more substantial.[93] Christian hospitality is not based upon a thin civility but rather a rich Gospel truth (1 Peter 4:8). Only as an outgrowth of sincere worship of Jesus Christ can true hospitality emerge. As noted previously, hospitality goes from the church to the stranger(s) as a gift in the same way the church originally received hospitality as a gift from God. The church acts as a conduit for this gift, which encompasses the truth of the Good News in a transformative welcome to strangers.

The theological and practical error of many contemporary churches involves a distortion of hospitality—cheapening it into a benign inclusivity.[94] The Gospel of Jesus Christ welcomes all sinners into His arms (John 3:16-17); that welcome includes a call to repent, be healed, and lead a changed life. The message of Jesus in Matthew 4:17 begins with

[93] Ibid., 26.

[94] Ibid., 43.

"Repent!" Trumpeting inclusivity as an end in itself exhibits a theological error of monumental proportions. Christian hospitality is rooted in transformation. It welcomes the stranger fully but that welcome initiates a process of change; the welcome is not the end or culmination of the new relationship; rather hospitality begins a gifting with the goal of becoming Christ-like. Jesus calls and that call includes expectations of transformation. Hospitality necessarily means speaking the truth in love—offering grace with the goal of redemption.[95] The Great Commission of Matthew 28:16-20 commands as much.

Inclusivity is a secular substitute for hospitality, but a poor, thin one that fails to provide real welcome. Whereas welcome points both the host and the guest to God, inclusivity points only to its own internal virtue.[96] That virtue fails to include a transcendent element or a submission to something greater than itself. The horizontal welcoming is not possible without the vertical welcome acting as an impetus. Once that vertical welcome is received by a community of faith, that community of faith may then open itself to welcome the stranger as is. This horizontal welcome puts the stranger in touch with the same transformation experienced by the community of faith through the gifting of God (Romans 15:7) so the welcomed stranger grows.

Newman continues her critique. As hospitality has a fundamental distinction from inclusivity, it also contrasts with diversity.[97] While each individual is different, under the cross of Jesus all individuals, no matter how distinct, find equality through omnipresent sinfulness. Jesus offers each individual grace, love, and redemption. Newman utilizes the ubiquitous *imago dei* to ground the universality of human depravity and God's offer of hospitality. This shared theology, tradition and practice unites hosts and strangers on a higher plane of being. Individual sinners become the body of Christ through Christian hospitality. Diversity is absorbed in the dynamic of God's reconciliation of humanity (a vertical relation) and the sanctification of sinners (a horizontal relation).

---

[95] Ibid., 144.

[96] Ibid., 188.

[97] Ibid., 33.

The church offers Christian hospitality freely to all. Accepting that hospitality fully entails transformation of the sinner. This is an order of welcome beyond mere inclusivity or the false idol of diversity. It is a model built upon the Gospel message of Jesus Christ.

Within a Christian context, affirming homosexual behavior fails to witness to the Good News of Jesus Christ by denying transformation; denying a welcome to gay persons also fails to witness to the Good News of Jesus Christ by denying hospitality. While these errors come from opposites ends of the theological spectrum, both fall short of a Christian testimony and embodiment. A partial gospel is no Gospel at all.

While my wife and I didn't know what God would have in store for us on that fall Sunday morning as we pulled into First Baptist at Centre and Bridge Sts. in Trenton, God did. God's purpose and grace lived through the welcome of that congregation. Their hospitality resonated with the love of Jesus. It moved us closer to Him.

Many evangelical churches have exhibited a fear of welcoming gay persons, wrongly conflating welcoming with affirmation. A community of faith cannot maintain biblical integrity without offering hospitality to those in need of the Gospel (John 12:26). Jesus calls us to view others as sinners to be redeemed, not as outcasts to be excluded. The practical and theological dilemma inherent in offering hospitality to gay persons seems to be boundaries. At what point does a welcome become an affirmation? Where are the limits of welcoming without repentance or change? Can a congregation welcome well while maintaining its theological convictions? This may be asked of all orthodox congregations, not simply evangelical churches.

Turn the page as we move to Welcoming Porous Boundaries.

Study Questions

1. Share about your first visit at your church?
2. How were you welcomed?
3. Have you ever felt excluded by a church? If so, how and why?

4. How does your church welcome outsiders into its midst?
5. Where does your church put up barriers to the entrance of others?
6. Would a gay person be welcomed at your church? How do you know?
7. Pray the doors of your church would always be welcoming. Commit to making that prayer a reality by the power of the Holy Spirit.

Chapter Six

Welcoming Porous Boundaries

At a church I served previously, there was a particular small group that got a lot of attention from staff. This group had been together for many years. They had some wonderful believers in this group—servants with caring hearts. The group had been together for so long they became closed off from the larger community. They recycled their stories, sharing them over and over. They had not welcomed new people into their midst or multiplied to create new small groups in years. Thus their internal dynamic had become unhealthy—unhealthy for the church itself and for those members.

Groups need some internal cohesion to become groups. This group had internal cohesion because they had lived life together, meeting weekly to share and pray. They had an internal group identity without a doubt. The whole congregation knew who was in it and by extension who was not. More on this to come.

Miroslav Volf provides a conceptual framework for offering welcome without losing the identifiable markers that make a community a community. However distinct individuals are from one another, including groupings of individuals, they share a universal need for rescue. Under the shroud of enmity, both the oppressed and their oppressors need liberation. This is an ontological truth. It is at our definable core. Jesus Christ provides that freedom through the cross.[98] The solidarity of humanity rests in both its sinfulness (Romans 3:23) and God's provision for salvation (John 3:16-17). Jesus Christ therefore provides a means to reinterpret who you are and how you connect with someone else.

---

[98] Miroslav Volf, *Exclusion and Embrace: A Theological Exploration of Identity, Otherness and Reconciliation* (Nashville: Abingdon Press, 1996), 25.

The self-giving of Christ [literally with arms nailed wide!!] offers both the hope of transformation to sinners and a stature to embody for His followers. The Cross presents communion, peace, and purpose; it also demands vulnerability and trust. Volf utilizes the image of embrace as a metaphor for initiating the welcome of others.[99]

Consider this. What is more inviting—walking toward someone who has a posture of welcome or someone in a stance with arms crossed? What is more welcoming—a smile or a blank face displaying apathy? What is more welcoming—an open hand to shake or a person with hands firmly pocketed? You know the answers to these. We've probably been on both sides of these encounters and sadly, probably while at church.

Recapping from chapter 5, embrace opens oneself to the other; it is a gesture of hospitality and solidarity. When I offer embrace to you, I open myself to you; I am vulnerable and literally exposed. I also exhibit a willingness to trust, if not you, then my God. When you embrace me, I encounter a greeting of safety. There is welcome and the offer of connection, both physical but more importantly relational. The act of embracing is an act of grace, modeled after Christ's gracious self-donation on the cross. Forgiveness, atonement, reconciliation and liberation are connected to truth and love. Embrace brings out this asymmetrical tie. Embrace does not begin with an accounting for offenses. It begins with welcome. As the embrace gives way to a more mature and deeper relationship, love and truth then come forward in tangible ways.

I love Volf's use of embrace as a sign of Jesus' welcome of the sinner to Himself, and the Church's welcome of sinners to Christ. Transpose embrace, both its image and meaning, to hospitality. This is welcoming. It is opening the door. It is offering others an opportunity to believe, belong and become. It is an invitation. It is saying come with me to church. Serve with me in this ministry. Let me tell you about Jesus Christ my Savior. Let me connect with you in a deep and personal way because you matter to me and you matter to Jesus.

Does embrace and hospitality amount to affirmation or inclusion of practices and ideas that contradict the practices and ideas of that

[99] Ibid., 29.

community? Can a community of faith offer embrace to those outside the community of faith without affirming behaviors of those outsiders? Are a church's internal boundaries oppositional to embrace?

The cultural drive towards inclusion and tolerance has as its goal the elimination of all boundaries and differences. Inclusion is not synonymous with embrace.[100] There are boundaries to embracing. There are markers for communities of faith and every community, necessarily. Boundaries do allow for embrace and connection. Boundaries allow for welcoming.

However, without boundaries, there is no intentional opening of oneself to welcome someone else. I can't welcome you to something unless I am part of that something. In welcoming you, I venture out of my group to nomad's land (speaking interpersonally) to invite you to my group. A community without boundaries is not a community. A community has definition, an ethos, something that unites those community members. The root of the word *community* is the same as our word *common*. The community holds something(s) in common that makes it a community to begin with.

This dynamic flagrantly contradicts the cultural and religious prophets of inclusion who see all boundaries as judgmental. On the one hand, these critics are correct in the boundaries are judgmental. They set who is inside and who is outside of them. On the other hand, this delineation isn't a weakness of communities but a necessity. Boundaries are an essential ingredients of being a community. That small group in Texas had strong internal cohesion through shared stories and experiences over many years.

Churches have boundaries. They have statements of faith. They have the Bible. They have internal polity and governance. They have members. They may have specific confessions to Jesus Christ as Lord. They may have practices that mark them distinctly. Those are all boundaries. And they are needed to define a church and the Church.

Churches do not exist as non-conditional uber-inclusive entities without boundaries. A group cannot call itself a community without naming those things that it holds in common or unity. In the case of congregations, that common unity is Jesus and the implications through scripture of what it

---

[100]. Ibid., 66.

means to follow Jesus. Volf notes the fatal flaw in thinking groups can exist sans internal structure:

> ***Without boundaries we will be able to know only what we are fighting against but not what we are fighting for. . .Intelligent struggle against exclusion demands categories and normative criteria that enable us to distinguish between repressive identities and practices that should be subverted and non-repressive ones that should be affirmed.***[101]

To provide an illustration of Volf's point, Alistar McGrath in Christianity's Dangerous Idea shares the story of the creation of an Independent Board of Foreign Missions in 1933 by J. Gresham Machen, a renowned fundamentalist. He formed this body with other like-minded Presbyterian clergy as an alternative to the Presbyterian Board of Foreign Missions, which in his opinion had become too ecumenical. Those other like-minded clergy were united only in their opposition to the Presbyterian Board of Foreign Missions; they could agree on virtually nothing else as it related to missions so their own Independent Board of Foreign Missions did nothing memorable other than to work against the Presbyterian Board of Foreign Missions.[102]

As a church, we are bound together by the blood of Jesus. We battle against the principalities and powers. The blood of Jesus is not repressive but liberating. The principalities and powers, the spirits of this world, are repressive and enemies of the fellowship of believers. Without the substance of common unity, the group is not a group but a random

---

[101] Ibid., 63. Here lies a valid critique of inter-faith work, which has inclusion as a primary focus. The groups that join together for inter-faith endeavors do so only to join together, not to truly know one another. Member organizations refrain from talking about who they are and/or what they are about among other member organizations for fear of offending or being offended by one another. In this joining together, the constituent organizations lose their uniqueness, identity and specificity. Inclusion here, rather than building connections that are strong enough to handle difference and distinction between member groups, offers a cheap substitute for true hospitality and welcome in the form of generic syncretism.

[102] Alistair McGrath, *Christianity's Dangerous Idea* (NY: Harper One, 2007), 394.

coincidence of people bumping into one another. Without Jesus and followers' calls to obedience, the church isn't a church. There are conditions to joining a church, to moving within it. This is true for virtually every group. These boundaries provide the safety of commonality within the group—we are brothers and sisters together. Because we have this common unity, we can go forth past the boundaries to welcome others.

Likewise, without that common unity, welcoming becomes meaningless. I don't welcome people into my neighbor's yard, because it isn't my yard. I can only welcome others and outsiders into my space. It is my space based on boundaries and conditions. Only because a church has polity and theological convictions, can it make an intentional effort to welcome others. That intentional effort of welcoming, like an individual embrace, exposes the church, makes it vulnerable and provides the opportunity for an encounter between the church and an outsider. Welcoming only happens if there is something to welcome the other to; in this case, a church offers hospitality to welcome others into community to meet and know Jesus Christ.

Within creation, Volf finds a Creator who separates and connects, pulls apart and brings together. Thus, differentiation and connection are necessary parts of societal organization and human relating. "We are who we are not because we are separate from the others who are next to us, but because we are *both* separate *and* connected, *both* distinct *and related*; the boundaries that mark our identities are both barriers and bridges."[103] Embrace therefore does not eliminate differences or boundaries. In welcoming someone to Jesus, gay persons for instance, I am not affirming homosexual behavior. I am welcoming someone to the embrace of Christ and Christ's people.

Those same boundaries provide conditions and opportunities for entrance into that community by others. There are ways for new people to join churches. There are welcome classes. There are outreach events. There are service opportunities. There are membership classes. Most churches have their doors open for any who want to join in Worship—just walk inside. There are on-ramps for outsiders who are not part of the church to

---

[103] Volf, 66. Author's italics.

become part of the community. I would gather you the reader have traveled these on-ramps to become part of your current church.

Going back to the small group from Texas referenced earlier in the chapter, they had boundaries. But they didn't have onramps for others to join. They didn't have mechanisms for new people to become part of the group. They liked their group; they knew each other's stories well; they had provided comfort and care to one another over many years. There is value to this certainly; but without onramps, the group suffocates. It becomes insulated. It is less a church or church small group but more akin to a cult. And that small group eventually disbanded with most leaving the church including some marriages breaking up. The boundaries became barriers rather than connections. The lack of onramps became stifling.

To offer a brief recap of this material, welcoming does not entail abject inclusion or blanket tolerance. Nor do church boundaries entail outright exclusion. In welcoming, a church opens itself to the unchurched, believers open themselves to non-believers. This embrace comes from the solidarity of universal sin and grace offered through Jesus Christ. The embrace does not entail assimilation or the loss of identity of the Church. Rather, through porous boundaries, the embrace offers the opportunity for a new relationship between believers and unbelievers while maintaining the distinctions of both parties.

Welcoming affords transformation. To use proximity as part of the embrace metaphor, when one enters embrace the two parties relocate position. The embracer and the embraced find a new location together while in the embrace. This new location shows the power of connection.[104]

Paul is a prime example of being embraced through his conversion in Acts 9:1-6. Paul's transformation from Saul didn't happen through some solitary or inward exercise. The change in him did not occur by an interior movement. Rather, Paul found a new identity outside himself through an encounter with the suffering Messiah Jesus Christ. The embrace of Christ offered this. Jesus re-named and re-made Paul. Jesus re-names and re-makes all followers. God models embrace in bringing sinful humanity into

---

[104] Ibid., *Exclusion and Embrace*, 71.

divine communion; this is the model for followers of God to utilize to bring others into fellowship.[105]

The church, to live out its call of obedience, must open its arms to sinners (1 Peter 4:11). It must extend an invitation to those who do not know Christ to enter into fellowship and discover liberation. Jesus did not offer tolerance; he demanded repentance. Christ did not hand over acceptance; he granted forgiveness. Forgiveness necessarily follows confession of and repentance for sin. Forgiveness is forgiveness for offenses. Welcoming love precedes these. The church, as the Body of Christ, provides hospitality in welcoming gay persons into a relationship. This relationship is a vehicle to bring sinners to Jesus for reconciliation and transformation.

Embrace does not amount to assimilation—no Borg here. It is not tacit affirmation. It is a welcoming, an offering of hospitality. The porous boundaries allow the church to maintain biblical and theological integrity while opening itself to a genuine and sincere relationship. Recipients of God's grace must become agents of that grace.[106] It begins with the embrace.

The parable of the Prodigal Son in Luke 15:11-32 provides illustration of this dynamic. The father did not need to hear the prodigal son's confession before embracing him because the embrace from the father was not based on the moral performance of the son.[107] It was a reception, an invitation, and a welcome return. By contrast, the older son failed to embrace his brother and thereby disconnected [un-son-ed] himself from the father. The younger son did not receive reinstatement to former privileges through the embrace; the porous boundaries provided admission but those boundaries remained in effect. Rather, the son received the ring of the father and the feast as acts of generosity; but all the property was and remained the older son's. The father reconfigured the order and embraced the younger son. The father didn't destroy the order nor did he exclude the

---

[105] Ibid., 72-73.

[106] Ibid., 129.

[107] Ibid., 159-161.

younger son. The only means for reconciliation was to offer embrace and thus encounter the other in a stance of openness. Relationships begin anew.

Embrace offers a biblical and theological model to provide connection and begin relationships without losing one's identity or opportunity for the other to experience transformation. Embrace offers a critical starting point for evangelical churches to provide hospitality to gay persons and thereby welcome them into fellowship with Jesus Christ. This embrace differs from affirmation and relies upon the transcendent power of Jesus Christ to transform.

The Church has an abysmal record in offering hospitality to gay persons. With rare exceptions, evangelical churches have not made a major or concerted effort to offer hospitality to gay persons. We are more known for taking dogmatic positions that lay out a biblical and theological stance against homosexual practice.[108] We have been more interested in winning argument points for ourselves than people for Jesus. Christians have demonized, ostracized and condemned gay persons for centuries.

The Westboro Baptists out of Arkansas provide the most obvious example in the United States. Some might argue this cult/church represents a caricature. Evangelical churches may not have picketed funerals for AIDS patients or protested with signs that read "God Hates Fags," but the lack of hospitality or welcoming initiative from churches to gay persons has subtly communicated a very similar message. In my opinion, evangelical churches—and I consider myself a pastor of an evangelical church—have much to repent for in this regard. Christian action, inaction, and callous rhetoric have driven those who might find transformation in the loving arms of Jesus Christ away from a community claiming to offer hospitable welcome to all (3 John 7-8).

As congregations seek to provide hospitality to gay persons, evangelical churches have a reputation and history of denunciation to overcome. In conversations with gay persons regarding their interaction with Christians and the church, Andrew Marin has found two common threads: grief and

---

[108] The recent Nashville Statement serves as a timely example. To read it in its entirety, see Appendix E.

visceral pain. Many gay persons feel alone in their search for God.[109] According to a recent survey, non-Christians have three primary perceptions of Christians: they are 1) anti-gay, 2) judgmental and 3) hypocritical.[110] This perception contrasts sharply with Peter's admonition to believers in 1 Peter 4:7-11.

The church is to welcome gay persons exactly as the church welcomes all persons (Hebrews 13:1-3).[111] The church is made up of sinners—sinners of all kinds. Purity—or any arbitrary standard of holiness—is not a requirement for admission (Matthew 9:9-13). The church is a refuge from the storms of life and a place of transformation; this is true for all who enter its doors; homosexuals are not an exempt class excluded from God's offer of healing.[112] No one comes to the church pristine or perfect (Romans 3:23); rather we come to the church to work out our salvation in "fear and trembling" within a community of others seeking to do the same (Philippians 2:12). The church is intended to be a place of gathering, not exclusion (Zechariah 11:16 and Luke 15:1-7). The church must ask, and help gay persons to answer, how believers with homosexual attraction may live in surrender and faithfulness to Jesus Christ.[113] Some churches have treated gay persons not unlike first century Jewish religious leaders treated tax collectors; Luke 19 serves as a reminder that Jesus welcomed Zacchaeus and even went to his house.[114]

Andrew Marin shares nine concerns that gay persons have of evangelical Christians: 1) relating to Christians in a church environment; 2) sexuality as the sole identifier in church; 3) invitation to church groups and activities; 4) concern that Christians think homosexuality is a special sin; 5) belief that being gay is a choice; 6) fear that friendship will be misinterpreted as flirtation; 7) fear of being labeled a pedophile; 8) fear of

---

[109] Marin, *Love is an Orientation,* 20.

[110] Ibid., 100.

[111] Grenz, *Welcoming but Not Affirming*, 2.

[112] Ibid., 133.

[113] Hill, *Washed and Waiting*, 16.

[114] Sprinkle, *People to Be Loved*, 77.

being labeled HIV positive; and 9) fear of being kicked out of the church.[115] The church must address these concerns with tact and love. Hospitality reminds believers that conversion is an act of God, not of humanity nor of the church. The willingness of a church to provide hospitality to gay persons centers upon love and welcome; the work of conviction, repentance and conversion remains under the auspices of the Holy Spirit.[116] If this list doesn't hurt your heart, get on your knees and pray for more truth and grace. We as believers must do better for the sake of those who need Jesus.

It is much easier to remain behind solid partitions than to allow openings for others to enter one's space, just as it is easier to cross one's arms than to open them wide for embrace. Those partitions may be barriers of brick and mortar or obstacles of words and practice. Having a completely defined space that delineates between those in and those out provides a simpler life. It is ungodly and against the missional command of Jesus but it is easier for like to just hang out with like. This describes a cult, not a church.

A church of porous boundaries demands effort and intention. From firsthand experience, it's hard. There are immense challenges. It takes much prayer, communication, and a lot of confession on one's knees. I know. We are called to this. The dynamic of faithfulness allows for the Holy Spirit to come forth, offering mutual transformation of the welcomed and welcomers, the stranger and the community (Galatians 5:13).

The issue for evangelical congregations fulfilling their mission to offer hospitality to all sinners concerns porous boundaries. Does Scripture provide assistance with working out porous boundaries? Does it offer a means to provide hospitality to gay persons without compromising the faith integrity of the community? Does the Bible offer limitations to the porous nature of congregational boundaries? Luke 15:1-3 and 1 Corinthians 5:9-13 may answer these questions.

Luke 15 contains one parable told three different ways: a lost sheep, a lost coin and a lost son. These images reinforce a single point—God rejoices over the salvation of lost sinners. The occasion that warrants these

---

[115] Marin, *Love is an* Orientation, 31-32.

[116] Ibid., 108.

images comes in verses 1-2. Jesus overhears the muttering of the religious leaders against him concerning his hospitality toward religious outcasts. The complaints against Jesus' fraternizing with tax collectors and sinners began in Luke 5:30. They are two-fold in nature: Jesus shows hospitality to these outsiders who by their sinfulness and impurity deserve none and Jesus dines with them. The Pharisees lumped tax collectors within the same category as robbers, evildoers and adulterers.[117] They failed to meet the holiness standards of the Mosaic law. They also failed to abide by the strict rules and regulations of the Pharisees themselves. They do not therefore deserve welcome nor hospitality until they repent and change their lifestyles. That Jesus would dine with these impure people only solidified the complaint. Table fellowship was an important part of Ancient Near Eastern culture. It was one thing to feed the downtrodden and sinners; it was quite another to dine with them. Sharing a meal implied acceptance and solidarity.[118] John the Baptist called sinners to repentance; Jesus dined with those same sinners. Jeremias writes: "[T]o invite a man to a meal was an honour. It was an offer of peace, trust, brotherhood and forgiveness . . . The inclusion of sinners in the community of salvation, achieved in table-fellowship, is the most meaningful expression of the message of the redeeming love of God."[119]

In response to grumbling of the Pharisees and keepers of the Law, Jesus offers a parable. The message of the parable is that God revels in the recovery of the lost. David Garland notes the objections to Jesus' inclusion of tax collectors and sinners was not the only cause for friction with the religious leaders; they also objected to the celebratory nature of Jesus' proclamation.[120] The religious caste sought to keep out the impure, the

---

[117] David Garland, *Luke*, Zondervan Exegetical Commentary on the New Testament (Grand Rapids: Zondervan, 2011), 611.

[118] Kenneth Bailey, *Poet and Peasant and Through Peasant Eyes: A Literary-Cultural Approach to the Parables in* Luke, Combined Edition (Grand Rapids: Eerdmans, 1983), 1423.

[119] Joachim Jeremias, *New Testament Theology: The Proclamation of Jesus* (New York: Scribner, 1971), 115f.

[120] Garland, *Luke*, 608.

irreligious, those who had made poor decisions and defiled themselves. The religious leaders exhibited a fear the impurity of sinners would somehow infect them and impact their own personal/communal holiness. Tax collectors and sinners had a religious 'leprosy' keeping them out of and away from holy people.

Jesus by contrast was not afraid of being tainted by his association with these outcasts. He sought out sinners to bring them into relationship with God, lacking any hesitation or concern that his own personal piety would suffer. The Pharisees avoided sinners and tax collectors. They understood repentance as a precondition for grace; in this chapter Jesus reorders salvation so that repentance occurs as a response to grace.[121]

Several points from this passage speak to porous boundaries. First, Jesus did not lower his standards toward sin by associating, hosting and eating with those the Pharisees excluded. He maintained a message of holiness and obedience. But, this message went forth to those most in need of it. Second, Jesus did not act as though his offer of hospitality to these sinners would negatively impact his relationship to God. Rather, he demonstrated the opposite. His relationship with God influenced and transformed many of those the Pharisees considered outside of God's love. Finally, Jesus sought out the lost by offering them hospitality; he did so without affirming their sin. Jesus modeled porous boundaries in seeking the lost. He maintained strict holiness and piety while allowing sinners and tax collectors to taste the Kingdom of Heaven.

In 1 Corinthians 5, Paul advocates the church in Corinth cast out a believer who was involved in an immoral relationship, arguing that continued association with this sinner will infect and damage the entire Corinthian church. Upon first reading, one might parallel Paul's stance with that of the Pharisees and keepers of the Law in Luke 15:1-2. Paul and Jesus are not at odds. 1 Corinthians 5:9-13 offers some clarity as to this issue and demonstrates that Paul's argument does not contradict Jesus' hospitality toward sinners but in fact follows that example.

---

[120] Bailey, *Poet and Peasant*, 155.

Following his admonition for the expulsion of the young man now sleeping with his father's wife, Paul specifies the audience of his argument. Paul argues the church must expel believers who act immorally because they sully the name of Christ and threaten the holy distinctiveness of the Christian community. Paul makes a distinction here between insiders and outsiders.[122] Insiders who call themselves Christian but act no differently from non-believers dilute the distinctiveness of the Christian community. The faith community is to send those nominal believers out of the community; this includes exclusion from table fellowship and the Lord's Supper. Outsiders who do not claim the name of Christ are not judged by the same standard as insiders. The faith community does not condemn non-believers for their behavior; rather the Christian community has the mission to share the Gospel with those non-believers.

Paul offers a first century contrast between the early church and the Qumran community. The Qumran followers withdrew from the world, seeking to place a geographic boundary between themselves and outsiders.[123] This boundary would preserve the holiness of the Qumran community from the impurity of the secular world around them. Paul finds this solution to the challenge of preserving pious distinction absurd and impossible. He does not advocate building a hard and firm barrier to keep out non-believers. He does expect Corinthian Christians to provide accountability to church insiders who live immoral lives for the sake of the unrepentant—to bring him to repentance—and for the sake of the church—to maintain its integrity to a Jesus-filled life.

The hard and fast boundaries that necessitate exclusion apply to believers within a believing community. Nominal Christians must leave the faith community. Their continued presence harms the larger community. Porous boundaries however remain for those outside the faith community,

---

122. Robert Hays, *First Corinthians*, Interpretation: A Bible Commentary for Teaching and Preaching (Louisville: John Knox Press, 2011), 87.

123 Hays, *First Corinthians*, 87.

including the "immoral, or the greedy and swindlers, or idolaters." To these, the Christian community offers hospitality and embrace.[124]

Luke 15 and 1 Corinthians 5 provide biblical foundations for porous boundaries. New Testament expulsions apply to lapsed believers, not to those outside the faith. The mandate to reach the lost continues. Hospitality then is as much a hallmark of Christian piety as is the prohibition against homosexual behavior found within Scripture. Porous boundaries provide the means to maintain the both/and dynamic of hospitality to gay persons and affirming biblical truth.

Church is the place for relationships built on grace and truth to grow and live. Through the offer of hospitality, gay persons may come to know transformation and comfort. Those offering hospitality may come to know love and correction are not mutually exclusive but instead are complementary.[125] Jesus offers a model for seeking relationships with gay persons—mutually transforming, deep and meaningful relationships. In this connection, evangelical believers and gay persons may come to know that the love of Jesus is neither permissive nor conditional.[126]

As one moves closer to the center of a church, the boundaries become firmer and less porous. Churches open doors for all to enter to worship. That is true at FBC Scottsdale. When people want to volunteer in certain areas, we require some background checks and references. Membership requires more agreement from the prospective member. There are additional boundaries to become a Deacon or Elder. And professional leadership has numerous policies and practices to agree and consent to before being hired. Expectations and community standards can become gates; not all on-ramps are quick or easy. This dynamic maintains the identity of the community.

---

[124] The practical work of determining where boundaries are and are not porous will depend in some part upon individual churches. Baptism, membership, leadership, communion and volunteering are all levels of participation. Subsequent chapters offer data upon these demarcations.

[125] Gagnon, *The Bible and Homosexual* Practice, 34.

[126] Sprinkle, *People to Be Loved*, 82.

A church with a theological foundation anchored to biblical truth—truth about the prohibition of homosexual behavior and the mandate to offer welcome—will exhibit boundaries strong enough to maintain a community's identity with Christ and porous enough to allow sinners and those in need of Jesus to come forward. In this way, the evangelical church may welcome gay persons into the embrace of Jesus Christ, the Son of God, while maintaining theological integrity. Welcoming demonstrates both love and truth.

Study Questions

1. What are the internal markers of your church as it related to boundaries?
2. What are the onramps for outsiders to become insiders of your church?
3. How strong are the boundaries?
4. How porous are the boundaries?
5. How would you welcome a gay person to your church?
6. How would others in your church welcome that same person?
7. Pray for your church and its welcome. Pray for your gay community and for God to bring these people into your doors. If you cannot pray for this, pray one day soon you will be able to.

Chapter Seven

Welcoming Practices

I have shared an orthodox theology of scripture, sexual ethics, and community. Having also gone through a lengthy explanation of the divine call to Jesus-followers to welcome all into a relationship with the Savior, I come to the key question, where the rubber hits the road so to speak. HOW TO GET YOUR CHURCH AND YOUR PEOPLE TO THIS PLACE?! We must show hospitality and hold close the theological conviction to welcome others into the arms of Jesus. Every church must find agreement on what exactly that welcoming entails to maintain its theological core. This chapter will provide a basis for your congregation to figure out its own porous boundaries.

To determine the rigidity and porousness of the boundaries, where the onramps are and are not, a congregation and/or minister must determine what boundaries secure the identity of the community. What openings allow a congregation to offer hospitality to gay persons in ways that do not threaten that faith community's theological integrity? You must balance what is too much, what is too little, and what Jesus wants from you/for you.

Yes—you read that right. I am not going to tell you what your porous boundaries should be. I am not going to list them. I am not going to say, do this one thing and you'll have it and it'll be great. Finding those boundaries that make your congregation what it is and finding the porous on-ramps within those boundaries, is distinct for each congregation. This process needs to include leadership, lay leadership and your congregation. If you plan to offer hospitality and welcome gay persons intentionally, you need buy-in. Buy-in costs. It costs time for conversations. It costs time for prayer. It costs education as to the what and why. If you plunked down the cost of this book and figured this amount would provide a total solution…um…no.

However, all the verbiage to this point has not been a tease. I will share with you a process to enter into these conversations with your professional leadership, lay leadership and congregation. I have used it. The prior chapters of this books are not only meant for reading but also for teaching. Walk your church or Deacons or small group or family through the material. Then get to the point or marking porous boundaries. That will be the toughest part.

Granted, it is easier to have general agreement on ideas and biblical concepts than it is to flesh those mandates out into actual practices. Remember, embrace makes us vulnerable. That's not easy. Keep going. This matters that much.

I wrote a survey to discern porous boundaries. The initial idea was to measure where those might be within specific churches. I gave this survey to 57 churches within my denominational region (American Baptist Churches of Los Angeles, the Southwest and Hawaii). The survey asked respondents to rate the receptivity of gay persons at their churches between (5) Strongly Disagree to (1) Strongly Agree at various levels of participation [you can find this survey in total in the Appendix B]. The second portion of the survey asked five open-ended questions regarding the church's position on homosexuality overall, how it arrived at that position and how this position has been communicated internally and externally to the congregation. The survey and results are in the graphic on the next page.

Church Survey					
	Strongly Agree	**Agree**	**Neither Agree nor Disagree**	**Disagree**	**Strongly Disagree**
1. My church has gay persons attending services	29%	24%	22%	16%	9%
2. My church would baptize a celibate gay person.	36%	29%	15%	11%	9%
3. My church would baptize a non-celibate gay person.	18%	6%	18%	18%	40%
4. My church would allow a celibate gay person to become a member of the congregation	35%	30%	17%	7%	11%
5. My church would allow a non-celibate gay person to become a member of the congregation.	18%	9%	18%	15%	40%
6. My church would hold a dedication service for the adopted biological child of a gay person.	17%	7%	30%	13%	33%
7. My church would allow a celibate gay person to serve as a church volunteer, such as participate in the choir.	34%	40%	11%	2%	13%
8. My church would allow a non-celibate gay person to serve as a church volunteer, such as participate in choir.	22%	13%	11%	25%	29%
9. My church would allow a celibate gay person to serve in church leadership, such as an elected board member.	26%	27%	22%	9%	16%
10. My church would allow a non-celibate gay person to serve in church leadership, such as an elected board member.	9%	6%	13%	17%	55%
11. My church would allow a staff member to conduct a gay wedding.	11%	2%	5%	20%	62%
12. My church would host a gay wedding.	9%	4%	5%	18%	64%

Of note, questions 7, 11, and 12 had the most agreement. Question 7 had 74% either "Strongly Agree" or "Agree." An additional 11% gave an ambivalent response. Only 15% answered this question regarding a celibate gay person volunteering negatively. Question 11 and 12 showed even greater agreement, though from a different perspective than Question 7. For Question 11, only 13% positively answered the query. 5% answered indecisively and 82% answered negatively. The results for Question 12 almost match those of Question 11. For Question 12, only 13% answered positively that their church would host a gay wedding. 82% answered either "Disagree" or "Strongly Disagree." A small sample, 5%, answered indecisively.

Also of note, questions 6 and 8 showed the most disagreement for respondents. Question 6's inclusion of an adopted child into the consideration of church practice toward gay persons illustrated the difficulty of making these decisions. 24% of respondents answered positively toward a child dedication; 30% were undecided; and 46% answered negatively. Question 8 showed more balance on both poles. Concerning the participation of a non-celibate person as a volunteer, 35% answered positively. 54% answered negatively. 11% answered ambivalently.

Some conclusions follow. First, celibacy both as an aspiration and description provides an important theological detail. The majority of surveyed churches focused upon behavior as opposed to orientation for gay persons. These churches expressed a willingness to allow the hypothetical celibate gay person to enter into all substratum of the congregation. This welcome dropped drastically and with increasing succession for non-celibate gay persons as the questions asked about interior layers within the church.

Second, this celibate aspect had relevance within the second section of the survey. The churches who are seeking to offer hospitality to gay persons without affirming homosexual behavior make the theological connection between the sin of homosexual behavior and other sinful behavior. Underlying this practical theological application is a deeper theological truth of the fallenness of all of humanity. While Christians confess to infractions and profess repentance, we are not perfected to righteousness in this life. The church is a gathering place for those who need Jesus, regardless of the type of offense. While scripture clearly denotes homosexual behavior as sinful, **far more attention** is given to offenses of greed, dishonesty and injustice. Connecting homosexual sin within the context of sin per se provided a larger context for congregants to take up hospitality without having that initiative morph into acceptance and affirmation of homosexual behavior.

Third, churches must intentionally and safely discuss this issue. For those that have had this conversation, the survey revealed the struggles inherent to the process. However, as was noted earlier, "[d]enial cannot work." Churches, pastors and lay leaders need assistance and guidance in how to do this well so as not to cause internal damage to themselves, ignite fear within the congregation, and/or quash hospitality. Denominations, associations and other ecclesial entities must provide assistance in this process.

Fourth, a number of respondents indirectly referred to the concept of *porous boundaries*. The references indicated both a need to theologically understand the concept as well as a means to put it into application.

I revised this survey [see Appendix C] for my own congregation and gave it to a group of lay leaders, lay members and staff twice. The first survey was cold, without any introduction or education to the subject matter specifically. After having gone through a study of the material presented in this book, they took the survey a second time.

The results from the first section of the survey are in the table below. The headings signify Strongly Agree [SA], Agree [A], Neither Agree Nor Disagree [N], Disagree [D] and Strongly Disagree [SD]. The left column provides each question. The adjacent rows provide the percentage of responses within the five categories. Within each cell under the top row are the percentages of the answers given. The top percentage within each cell is the percentage answered at the first taking [T1] of the survey during Session One. The middle percentage signifies the percentage of answers after they retook the survey [T2]. The bottom percentage represents the change in percentages from the first taking to the second. These figures are in bold.

1. Our church has gay persons attending services	**T1**	**40%**	**27%**	**27%**	**6%**	**0%**
	T2	**73%**	**27%**	**0%**	**0%**	**0%**
	Change	**33%**	**0%**	**-27%**	**-6%**	**0%**
2. Our church would baptize a celibate gay person.	T1	27%	40%	20%	13%	0%
	T2	60%	40%	0%	0%	0%
	Change	**33%**	**0%**	**-20%**	-13%	**0%**
3. Our church would baptize a non-celibate gay person.	T1	6%	40%	20%	6%	27%
	T2	27%	33%	13%	20%	6%
	Change	**21%**	**-7%**	**-7%**	**13%**	**-21%**
4. Our church would allow a celibate gay person to become a member of the congregation	T1	40%	47%	6%	6%	0%
	T2	67%	27%	6%	0%	0%
	Change	**27%**	**-20%**	**0%**	**-6%**	**0%**
5. Our church would allow a non-celibate gay person to become a member of the congregation.	T1	13%	33%	20%	20%	13%
	T2	33%	47%	6%	13%	0%
	Change	**20%**	**14%**	**-13%**	**-7%**	**-13%**
6. Our church would hold a dedication service for the adopted biological child of a gay person.	T1	13%	27%	20%	27%	13%
	T2	13%	13%	20%	40%	13%
	Change	**0%**	**-14%**	**0%**	**13%**	**0%**
7. Our church would allow a celibate gay person to serve as a church volunteer, such as participate in the choir.	T1	27%	33%	13%	13%	13%
	T2	20%	53%	13%	13%	0%
	Change	**-7%**	**20%**	**0%**	**0%**	**-13%**
8. Our church would allow a celibate gay person to serve in church leadership, such as an elected board member.	T1	0%	27%	33%	20%	20%
	T2	6%	27%	13%	27%	40%
	Change	**6%**	**0%**	**-20%**	**-7%**	**20%**
9. Our church would allow a staff member to conduct a gay wedding.	T1	13%	0%	6%	33%	47%
	T2	0%	0%	13%	27%	60%
	Change	**-13%**	**0%**	**7%**	**-6%**	**13%**
10. Our church would host a gay wedding.	T1	6%	0%	13%	27%	53%
	T2	0%	0%	0%	33%	67%
	Change	**-6%**	**0%**	**-13%**	**6%**	**13%**
11. A gay person would be welcome at our church.	T1	47%	40%	6%	6%	0%
	T2	67%	27%	0%	0%	0%
	Change	**20%**	**-7%**	**-6%**	**-6%**	**0%**
12. A gay person would be welcome at any Worship service at our church.	T1	40%	47%	6%	6%	0%
	T2	60%	27%	0%	6%	6%
	Change	**20%**	**-20%**	**-6%**	**0%**	**6%**
13. A gay person would be welcome at our church.	T1	33%	40%	13%	13%	0%
	T2	47%	40%	0%	6%	6%
	Change	**14%**	**0%**	**-13%**	**-7%**	**6%**
14. A gay person would be welcome at any Serve Team at our church.	T1	13%	40%	20%	20%	6%
	T2	20%	6%	33%	27%	13%
	Change	**7%**	**-34%**	**13%**	**7%**	**7%**
15. I would invite a gay friend/neighbor/co-worker to our church.	T1	27%	47%	13%	6%	6%
	T2	53%	47%	0%	0%	0%
	Change	**26%**	**0%**	**-13%**	**-6%**	**-6%**
16. I do not see any hindrances to a gay person feeling welcome at our church.	T1	0%	47%	27%	27%	0%
	T2	6%	40%	20%	27%	6%
	Change	**6%**	**-7%**	**-7%**	**0%**	**6%**

There are several findings from this data. Per questions 2, 3, and 4, the group acquired a working theology that offers hospitality to gay persons at First Baptist Church, Scottsdale, Arizona, through porous boundaries. Celibacy clearly mattered in terms of involvement within the church. Answers to questions 9 & 10 illustrate the limits of these openings as hospitality gives way to expected transformation. Question 14 shows continued confusion as to First Baptist Church's porous boundaries with a wide dispersion of responses. I have more work to do in this area to get us to a position of clarity. This is a good reminder the work doesn't cease.

Beginning with survey question 17, section two of the survey asked six open-ended queries. Question 17 asked *How would you characterize First Baptist Church, Scottsdale, Arizona's position on homosexuality?* The responses from the Session One surveys included the following: "that they are probably welcome"; "I don't really know"; "this is largely unknown to me"; "silent"; and "ambiguous".

The responses garnered from the re-taking, after a period of study, included the following: "not accepting but welcome them"; "chooses the Bible as its final authority"; "it is sin"; "welcome a person with an understanding that we are all growing closer to Christ"; and "porous boundaries".

Question 18 asked *What has been the greatest difficulty within First Baptist Church, Scottsdale, Arizona, surrounding homosexuality?* The responses from the first taking included the following: "lack of clarity"; "ambiguity"; "addressing it head on"; "the silence"; and "ignorance".

The responses from the second taking included the following: "boundaries"; "clarity…what we allow"; "ignorance"; "conflict between biblical truth and biblical mandate to be hospitable"; "silence"; and "an avoidance of the issue".

Question 19 asked *How might First Baptist Church, Scottsdale, Arizona, offer hospitality to a gay person?* The responses from the initial survey included the following: "openness to their participation"; "I don't know"; and "we need to be open, honest, and biblically sound about our position on this".

The responses from the second taking after studying the issue included the following: “the same way we offer hospitality to everyone”; “welcome them”; and “building relationships”.

Question 20 asked *How might you offer hospitality to a gay person?* The responses from the first taking included the following: “same as anyone else”; “show grace”; and “break bread with them”.

The responses from second taking included the following: “interact”; “like I would anyone”; “listening to their journey”; and “build genuine friendship”.

Question 21 asked *What makes First Baptist Church, Scottsdale, Arizona, hospitable to gay persons?* The responses from the first survey included the following: “not sure it is particularly”; “welcoming culture”; “an attitude of love and openness”; “the fact that we recognize our brokenness”; and “come as you are”.

The responses from the re-taking included the following: “no one is asked to disclose sins to attend”; “clear understanding on what the Bible says about hospitality”; “not there yet but trying”; and “we believe that God loves people, all people”.

Question 22 asked *What hinders gay persons from finding hospitality at First Baptist Church, Scottsdale, Arizona?* The responses from the initial survey included the following: “stereotype of a Baptist church”; “fear of not being welcome”; “there aren’t any here”; “the church’s reluctance to come forward and address the issue”; “lack of clarity leads to mixed messages”; and “I don’t know”.

The responses from the second taking included the following: “fear of being rejected”; “that a gay lifestyle is incompatible with biblical teachings”; “ability to grow with the church”; and “ignorance”.

Additionally, I recorded comments from participants during the study sessions. There was unanimous consensus that the Bible prohibits homosexual behavior. The Vimeo *Dear Church, I’m Gay* by Preston Sprinkle elicited a great deal of feedback and fostered greater awareness of the complexity of the issue and struggle involved with it from all sides [Sprinkle is to be commended for such thoughtful, in-depth work]. This video was mentioned as having broadened their understanding of the church's exclusion of gay persons and lack of hospitality shown to gay persons in the past.

I facilitated a time for final thoughts, just before the survey was re-taken. One participant said the church has had a "grand lack of clarity" on this issue. The study helped her gain a biblically founded perspective. Another noted it is not our "job to judge but to invite and let the Holy Spirit work." Amen brother!

Here are takeaways from the exercise, inclusive of both surveys and the study in between. First, the concept of celibacy and its theological implications became more prominent after the study. Based upon the change in percentages between the first and second taking of the survey, celibate gay persons would encounter very few barriers to full church participation. The exceptions to this trend concerned serving in church leadership and on serve teams [serve teams is the nomenclature used for missions and outreach]. It is possible these exceptions have to do with public representation of the church rather than internal hesitation. This demands more study and education on my part for the congregation.

Second, the desire and mandate to invite gay persons to church and welcome them once they come increased significantly between survey takings. The idea hospitality is a biblical mandate seemed to have an effect upon the overall attitude and welcoming application of the study group.

Third, pairing hospitality with a discussion of homosexuality, including exegesis of passages related to both, changed the dynamic of the discussion. One participant noted that too often a discussion of homosexuality devolves into heterosexuals telling gay persons what God doesn't want them to do. The hospitality aspect corrected this expected course. Hospitality provides a biblical and necessary mandate for heterosexuals. This alters the discussion so that everyone has investment in relationships.

Fourth, the discussion time during the sessions proved fruitful. The sessions provided safe space for the expression of a variety of opinions. Consensus was made on several aspects of this subject. Even with some divergent opinions [in keeping with Baptist polity], the disagreement was respectful. Amid minor disunity of thought, the group showed unity of purpose and proclamation.

The study achieved its purpose in seeking to answer questions of boundaries and openings, essentially, what porous boundaries look like for a congregation seeking to adhere to the biblical truth of prohibitions of homosexual behavior and commands for hospitable welcome. Celibacy matters and essentially functions as a means for porous boundaries. The discussion of homosexuality must include study of Christian hospitality; this provides flexibility and strength for the congregation. Congregations cannot ignore the issue as it pervades the culture, families, and most church pews.

Pastoral leadership is essential in navigating this process for congregations. In my role within the intervention group, I facilitated the discussion. I deferred when asked direct questions concerning my thoughts on the matter. It is possible, and likely, if I had served in a more active role the final survey results would have appeared differently. As a Baptist, pastors are not the sole arbiters of church doctrine or practice. However, pastors should have a place in leading a healthy discussion of the biblical prohibition toward homosexuality and the biblical mandate toward hospitality.

Feel free to utilize the survey for your own congregations and faith groups. It provides an easy way to begin the conversation, and to see where there are openings for the entirety of the Gospel message (truth and love) while the rest of the book provides the study content to make use of those openings. The study questions at the end of each chapter may help. I encourage you, knowing your groups better than I do, to add your own. Context is critical to your people.

Also, **listen** to your people. The goal is not to run them over with a theological *tour de force*. If they have hearts for Jesus, they will develop hearts for gay persons! It may take time. It will involve being uncomfortable. That's part of the process. Trust the Holy Spirit to work.

Study Questions

1. Take the survey in Appendix C.
2. Discuss the results as a group. What surprised you? What encouraged you? What work remains for you and your church on this issue?
3. Pray that God would strengthen your church and lead you to a place where you welcome all sinners into your midst and into the embrace of our Savior.

Conclusion

Welcoming

I have sought to provide a pathway by which Bible-believing churches can show hospitality to gay persons in order to facilitate a climate of transformation for those persons. While I would hope to change the minds of those clergy and believers who have implicitly (or explicitly) rejected the Bible's clear denunciation of homosexual behavior, this is not my goal. The theological left has erroneously determined that the Bible is wrong or irrelevant or both, at least in its references to homosexual behavior. The need for clarity of thought and explication of the doctrines of creation and redemption remains. The call to submit to something beyond our own individual (and at times communal) desires continues to sound. The questions asked in this project are not new; many have sought to reconcile how to love sinners while hating sin. Casting the divine initiative within the context of hospitality may be new.

Is failure of exegesis a greater ecclesial sin than a failure of invitation? Is lack of clarity concerning major doctrines worse than a lack of clarity concerning with whom Jesus would fellowship? The church, and its constituting members of both the theological left and right, have much to confess. As the left has failed to speak biblical truth to gay persons by affirming homosexual behavior, the right has failed to speak love to those same gay persons through hospitality. Until the evangelical church takes up its call to offer welcome, invitation and hospitality to gay persons under the larger rubric of offering those to **all** sinners, then it will fail to fulfill the Great Commandment (Matthew 22:36-40) and the Great Commission (Matthew 28:16-20).

How might evangelical churches utilize embrace to offer hospitality to gay persons? How can churches understand the necessary requirements of hospitality to welcome those different from themselves while also maintaining the biblical and theological integrity of their community of faith? How may faith communities set porous boundaries to welcome gay persons while insuring the cohesion of the community itself? Many churches have struggled to live out their call faithfully: remaining true to the scriptural warrant as it comes to homosexual behavior while answering Jesus' mandate to welcome sinners.

As stated in the introduction, my relationship with Jesus Christ informs me the message of the Gospel is for all; the message of the Gospel can sufficiently redeem all; and, the message of the Gospel must be shared with all. The same Bible that prohibits homosexual behavior also commands believers offer hospitality to sinners (Mark 12:30-31). The same Bible that commands hospitality also offers transformation from who we are—sinners—to who God intends us to be—redeemed disciples (Romans 12:2). I do not believe God set up an impossible dilemma for churches as it comes to gay persons. Many churches have made a false choice; some choose to ignore the scriptural truth prohibiting homosexual behavior; others choose to ignore the imperative to welcome gay persons to the message of Christ.

There was one particular insight I gained through the distribution of surveys to other churches that I had not expected. I expected criticism from the theological left; the point of this project was not to call them into biblical truth about homosexual behavior, though that would be a wonderful ancillary good. Rather, this project sought to call the evangelical church into the biblical practice of hospitality. I did not expect the criticism from the theological right as it related to hospitality toward gay persons. Some on the theological right reacted to the ABCOFLASH survey with suspicion and disgust over the issue of welcoming gay persons even being raised. Others of a like mind rejected hospitality to gay persons outright, offering welcome hypothetically only after those sinners repent and sufficiently redeem themselves. Some refused to participate.

I find this unexpected insight tragic. Redemption is found within the arms of Christ alone (Romans 3:23-25). Christians are to be conduits to Christ, not obstructive barriers. The reaction noted above only illustrates the need for a theological grounding in hospitality and its application—presented within this project through the concept of porous boundaries.

The Bible prohibits homosexual behavior without equivocation. The Bible also mandates hospitality toward sinners for the purpose of bringing those sinners into a redeeming relationship with Jesus Christ. The church has a mission and responsibility to speak truth and offer grace (2 Corinthians 4:13-15). Theologically constructed porous boundaries offer a means to do this.

Porous boundaries come only through intentional and specific study. Pastoral and lay leadership must set a course to move congregants into a theological understanding of the biblical truth about hospitality and homosexuality. Once the congregation has the theological foundation set, it may begin to talk about what welcoming gay persons into a relationship with Jesus Christ looks like within that church's context. As with most ministry, congregations will make missteps; these unintentional errors could prove harmful to the congregation itself, to gay persons through a poor witness of Gospel hospitality, or both. But churches can correct errors of practice. It's harder to correct an error of heart. Failing to welcome those in need of Jesus is more than an unintentional error; it is sin.

Understanding hospitality as participation with Jesus Christ, worship of Jesus Christ and finally commanded by Jesus Christ, will provide a congregation with the indicative necessary to move toward the imperative of offering hospitality (Matthew 28:19). Christians may only offer hospitality because they have first received it from God (Romans 12:1-2). Current members of the church did not deserve God's welcome; they did not earn God's embrace; yet through grace and love, God extended hospitality to each of them (Ephesians 2:8). The church therefore is God's house; God is always and ever present as its Host to all (Ephesians 2:19-22).

Living out one's faith in hospitality entails actively looking for opportunities to engage and welcome gay persons into a church. This manifests itself as receptivity to gay persons entering a congregation for worship. It comes alive as personal invitations for gay persons to join worship, small groups or other church activities. It is a mandate for a community of faith and individual believers. A church is expected to seek these occasions to connect and grasp them wholeheartedly (Mark 1:32-34, 1:40-42, Luke 5:27-32, and 15:8-10 to name a few). The charge to do this begins with pastoral leadership teaching and modeling to a congregation how to love and provide hospitality to gay persons.[127]

Having heard the charge from church leadership, the laity may adopt hospitality as a vocation. There are some easy bridges that evangelical churches can make with gay persons, including education to dispel misunderstandings about homosexuality, understanding the biblical function of hospitality as it relates to homosexuality, and committing to serve God through welcoming gay persons.[128] A church that is ready to welcome gay persons into its midst—into God's loving embrace—may start with this both to test its convictions as well as its practices. Richard Rohr reminds us changing paradigms, as this does, only happens when we live it out: we can't "think ourselves into new ways of living, we live ourselves into new ways of thinking."[129]

Hospitality implies joyous reception and an eagerness to engage. Expect these occasions. When gay persons show up or receive a proper welcome, the church must celebrate and rejoice! [130] This is an integral part of hospitality and readiness.

Hospitality inherently carries risk. As Jesus welcomed believers unto himself, he risked and ultimately gave his life (Mark 3:1-6). As the church opens its doors and leaves its familiar confines to actively seek out gay persons, there is uncertainty and anxiety. Opening one's arms to embrace another leaves the host exposed and vulnerable. The host also risks rejection if those welcomed refuse to enter the host's space.

There will be successes and there will be failures. This type of risk is not well managed; but it may be well experienced. Will a congregation risk mistakes? Will a congregation bear rejection? Will a congregation remain in a stance of embrace knowing embracing the other will result invariably in change of that congregation and a repositioning of one's stance or place?

---

[127] Chad Thompson, *Loving Homosexuals as Jesus Would* (Grand Rapids: Brazos Press, 2004), 11.

[128] Thompson, *Loving Homosexuals as Jesus Would*, 62-63.

[129] Grant, 216, from Richard Rorty, *Everything Belongs: The Gift of Contemplative Prayer* (NY: Crossroad, 2003), 19.

[130] Marin, *Love is an Orientation*, 79.

Without a fair assessment of this risk, even as the risk specifics are undefined, a congregation may shrink from porous boundaries and instead react to the inherent difficulty of the mandate of hospitality by insulating itself. Entering upon this path of hospitality carries risk.

As well, the faith community risks its identity when it welcomes outsiders. Porous boundaries must allow for strangers to enter; the identity of a community must have some elasticity to make room for new people. Inherent identity must also retain strength so the community is not overwhelmed by the welcomed. The boundaries must hold. Welcoming outsiders risks this tension—both the porous openings and the firmness of the boundaries. Exceptions to a community's rule—its theology and practice—do not truly threaten that community unless those exceptions become the rule.[131] A congregation that does not have a theological and biblical basis including the why and what of hospitality risks both its welcome to gay persons and its own identity.

The end of hospitality is not to be hospitable; it is to bring others into a relationship with Jesus Christ (Acts 17:27). Let me restate that. We do not welcome simply to welcome. We welcome others not to ourselves or our communities but to the Savior of the World. Hospitality is not constructed of finite occasions; it is an ongoing enterprise. Offering welcome does not stop. Its frequency does not end. Its depth continues. The Gospel compels the evangelical church to enter into deep connections with gay persons. This means the evangelical church can no longer view gay persons as caricatures or two-dimensionally.[132] This will only happen as the church views gay persons as sons and daughters of God, people God desperately wants to reach and redeem. For this to function, believers must know gay persons. This may happen through living life together, sharing in the ups and downs and the struggles and celebrations of living under a gracious God in a fallen world. Here the mutuality of knowing and being known, embracing and being embraced, come to fruition. The connecting builds

---

[131] Stanley Hauerwas, "Gay Friendship: A Thought Experiment," *Theology and Sexuality: Classic and Contemporary Readings*, ed. Eugene Rogers (Malden, MA: Blackwell Publishers, 2002), 301.

[132] Marin, *Love is an Orientation*, 21.

lasting relationships; it is not evangelism or conversion; it is friendship and bonding. The purpose of hospitality is to build horizontal and vertical relationships.[133] This means connecting lives, not moments. Jesus Christ builds his kingdom through relationships.

This project, as with many courses of study that demand both great time and attention, comes from a personal place. I want D., G., T., and others to have Christian community that will love them, support them in their struggles, and provide a witness to Jesus in their lives. The church is a place for sinners to come and be transformed through the power of Christ (1 Timothy 1:12-16). It has always been that for me; it may be that for gay persons. There is profound tension and real human pain as the church seeks to navigate a path that upholds biblical integrity and Christian hospitality for gay persons. Only by finding and following this path will the church become a place of redemption and liberation for all God's people as it was intended to be.

I want the Bride of Christ to welcome **all** into its midst. I want to lead First Baptist Church, Scottsdale, Arizona, into a place of porous boundaries so we may show hospitality to all people, including and intentionally gay persons. By this, First Baptist Church, Scottsdale, Arizona, may provide a home for D., G., T. and others so they may grow in their faith and relationship with God. By this, Christ will grow First Baptist Church, Scottsdale, Arizona, in its faith and relationship with God.

I want this for your church too. Far more importantly, Jesus wants this for all His churches.

---

[133] Marin, *Love is an Orientation*, 59.

Appendix A

Biblical Exegesis of Passages Referencing Homosexuality

There is no shortage of exegesis on the six passages that relate to homosexuality. I have included within this appendix the best scholarship of these verses, in my humble opinion.

Genesis 19:1-29

Within the context of the cycle, this passage details the contrast between depraved humanity and faithful Abraham. These verses also garner the most controversy as to their applicability to the project discussion. Hays argues that the passage has nothing to do with a prohibition of homosexual behavior and is thus irrelevant to the debate.[134] The sin of Sodom detailed here exceeds mere sexual sin; the sexual sin referenced, in this case intentional gang rape of males by males, highlights violence and the rejection of the cultural mandate to provide hospitality to strangers. Hays cites the other biblical references to Genesis 19 to bolster his position: Ezekiel 16:49-50 and 2 Peter 2:6-7. Ezekiel does not explicitly mention sexual sins within the list of Sodom's transgressions. Jude 7 does explicitly name sexual infractions as a cause for judgement, though homosexuality is not stated specifically. Outside of this verse in Jude, Hays finds nothing of use for the homosexuality discussion within Genesis 19 itself or within the other two references to Genesis 19.

Sprinkle agrees, noting that this has nothing to contribute to the discourse on consensual homosexual behavior.[135] Vines agrees with Hays

[134] Hays, *The Moral Vision of the New Testament*, 381.

[135] Sprinkle, *People to be Loved*, 42.

and Sprinkle. The issue in Genesis 19 concerns gang rape; homosexuality is an ancillary feature to the intended degradation of the angelic strangers visiting Lot.[136]

Gagnon makes the opposite case arguing that homosexuality is a prominent feature of this passage. The degrading nature of homosexuality adds an element of shame to the violence intended upon the visitors by the male citizens of Sodom.[137] Gang rape is a main component of the passage. Homosexuality, whether consensual or coerced, is a main component of that gang rape and should not be overlooked.

The verb in 19:5 translated in the NIV as "can have sex" comes from the Hebrew word *yada,* יָדַע, which means to know intimately. The NRSV translates this as "may know them." In contrast to some other commentators including Boswell, Gagnon argues that this knowing refers to sexual behavior explicitly in accord with the NIV translation. Gagnon reads *yada* as pointing to homosexual sin within the larger sin of gang rape. The perversion of homosexual behavior is a key element of this story. Brueggemann argues that *yada* does not usually refer to homosexuality, citing its use in Judges 19:22-25 for evidence.[138]

Hamilton notes that *yada* and its derivatives occur 1,058 times in the Old Testament. The verb form is used 948 times; 15 of these refer to knowing within a sexual context. In the other instances of *yada*, abuse and violence are not connoted in its usage.[139] Hamilton, utilizing verse 8, argues that homosexuality does play a part in this given the force of Lot's offer of his daughters. The rejection of them indicates that sexual intercourse per se is not the issue. The men want to have sex with these visiting men, not simply have sex per se.

Disputing Hays, Gagnon argues that Ezekiel 16:49-50 posits the sin of Sodom as homosexual behavior explicitly in verse 50 with the word "detestable" which comes from the Hebrew *tow'ebah*, תּוֹעֵבָה. This noun

---

[136] Vines, *God and the Gay Christian*, 65.

[137] Via and Gagnon, *Homosexuality and the Bible*, 71.

[138] Brueggemann, *Genesis*, 164.

[139] Hamilton, *The Book of Genesis*, 33-34.

may also be translated as "abomination." He interprets this as a reference to homosexual behavior. Likewise, he reads 2 Peter 2:7 and the Greek *aselgeia*, ἀσελγείᾳ, as inclusive of homosexual behavior in its translation as "sensuality." Jude 7 makes explicit the sexually sinful component of Sodom including an explicit reference to perversion, referring to homosexuality according to Gagnon.[140]

This passage, in distinction from the other five that follow, presents the most ambiguity. I believe that Gagnon's more expansive interpretation of the sins of Sodom fits the context better than other interpretations and adds to the gravity of its transgressions. However, the point of the story is not primarily to argue against homosexual behavior. The pendulum of scholarship once held that this passage was about little else. Then the pendulum swung so that homosexuality had nothing to do with this passage. The proper interpretation in my opinion lies in the middle. The story concerns human wickedness and divine wrath. Homosexuality is a part of that wickedness and thus a cause of that wrath. But, homosexual behavior is not the primary agent for God's judgement here. This text therefore is not a primary text for the discussion of the prohibition of homosexual behavior. It may serve as a secondary text.

Leviticus 18:22

Hays, Sprinkle and Gagnon all conclude that this verse explicitly rejects homosexual behavior without qualification or condition and do so absolutely.[141]

Vines asks the question why only male-male sexual behavior is condemned and not female-female sexual behavior here.[142] His question seeks to undercut the view that homosexual behavior per se is prohibited and instead offer a counter that scripture directs this prohibition against a specific occasion of homosexual behavior, offering the suggestion that the

---

[140] Gagnon, *The Bible and Homosexual Practice*, 58.

[141] Hays, *The Moral Vision of the New Testament*, 381. Sprinkle, *People to be Loved*, 45. Via and Gagnon, *Homosexuality and the Bible*, 63.

[142] Vines, *God and the Gay Christian*, 90.

Levitical writer aims this prohibition against Israelites participating in male cultic prostitution. However, ancient Israel was a patriarchal society. Women lacked the liberty to engage in homosexual behavior at will. This verse did not have to address lesbian behavior because lesbian behavior was outside the realm of possibility at that time. Sprinkle argues against this verse having anything to do with male cultic prostitution because of the unconditional force of the verse itself. The issue here is not participating in idol worship through homosexual practice but rather the prohibition of homosexual practice itself.[143]

Leviticus 18-20 is an expansion of the Ten Commandments from Exodus 20. Chapter 18 details forbidden sexual relations. These include adultery, incest and bestiality [child sacrifice does not fall within sexual sins but is mentioned as an abomination before God in this chapter]. This verse is part of the Holiness Code in Leviticus. This code set out markers for Israel's distinctiveness and specificity from other Canaanite peoples, both in identity and practice.

Gagnon argues that 18:22b illustrates a level of revulsion beyond what one might expect from other infractions.[144] This additional clause appears almost as commentary to the preceding prohibition, marking a deeper level of disgust with this practice. Given that the Holiness code is designed to sanctify Israel, this prohibition details personal, communal and spiritual degradation that occurs in male homosexual behavior. Hays asks the question on behalf of the church whether the Holiness Code is purity law or moral law? And if it is purity law, does Christ's justification of sinners then impact the church's understanding of these verses?[145]

This verse is specific and absolute. The secondary clause also increases the weight of this verse. Those who argue that this seemingly absolute prohibition is tailored only to a specific cultic practice do not have the weight of the evidence on their side.

---

[143] Sprinkle, *People to be Loved*, 46-47.

[144] Gagnon, *The Bible and Homosexual Practice*, 113-116.

[145] Hays, *The Moral Vision of the New Testament*, 382.

Leviticus 20:13

This verse is similar in substance to Leviticus 18:33 with one very notable exception. This verse includes the death penalty for the parties involved in this transgression. It is categorical in its rejection of male-male homosexual practice. It is also absolute in its punishment.

Gagnon notes that this penalty was unusual within the context of other ancient near eastern cultures. In other societies contemporary to early Israel, the punishment for male-male homosexual behavior was castration; it was not death. The Holiness Code of Leviticus 18-20 rejected many Canaanite practices explicitly. In this case, Israel's societal norms not only align with the other cultures surrounding them, the punishment for transgressing that norm exceeds that of the cultures around Israel.[146] He notes that the commentary clause regarding the detestable nature of the sin is also without parallel in other Canaanite legal codes.[147]

Kaiser raises the point that the punishment here is deemed perfectly just. The scales are balanced; the sentence fits the crime according to the Holiness Code.[148] The text itself makes this pronouncement. If there is shock over the judgement, it does not come from the text itself. As the sentence does not include additional verbiage to justify its capital punishment, one may presume that the original hearers would not have heard this sentence as unfair or unjust.

As with Leviticus 18:33, this verse does not mention female-female homosexual behavior. Gagnon offers this reasoning. Sexual intercourse at this time was defined primarily as penetration. With penetration as the qualifier, female-female homosexual behavior would not rise to the level of detestable activity.[149] The absence of an explicit reference to female-female homosexual behavior does not imply an endorsement of those

---

[146] Gagnon, *The Bible and Homosexual Practice*, 113-114.

[147] Ibid., 156.

[148] Walter C. Kaiser, Jr., *Leviticus*, New Interpreter's Bible: Genesis to Leviticus, Volume 1 (Nashville: Abingdon Press, 1994), 1142.

[149] Ibid., 144.

practices. It simply means that the writer had male-male homosexual behavior in mind per the cultural definition of intercourse at that time.

The penalty marks Leviticus 20:13 from its companion verse in Leviticus 18:33. The extreme and final nature of the penalty increases the gravity of this prohibition. Homosexual behavior warranted permanent expulsion of the practitioners from their community and from every community through a death sentence. Gagnon's research on homosexual prohibitions within other Canaanite communities may surprise Bible readers. I grew up with the idea that non-Israel cultures promoted sexual libertinism. The evidence says this was not true concerning homosexual behavior. All of Israel's neighbors had legal codes denoting male-male homosexual behavior as criminal. As notable, the punishment detailed in Leviticus 20 for the Israel community exceeded the punishment for this behavior codified among Israel's neighbors. The Holiness Code distinguishes Israel from its neighbors where there are distinctions to be made. Here, there is agreement upon the danger of homosexual practice in clear and unambiguous language and an excess in prescribed punishment.

Romans 1:26-27

These verses occur within the larger pericope of Romans 1:18-32. That pericope occurs within a cohesive section in which Paul makes a theological argument about depraved humanity and humanity's inability to become righteous: 1:18 – 3:26. Given the placement of Romans 1:26-27 within a sophisticated theological argument about human sinfulness and unrighteousness, this passage may provide a more thorough explanation for the rejection of homosexual behavior than the other passages that refer to homosexuality. Hays suggests that this is the most crucial text for determining what the Bible says about homosexuality; Wright likens this section to a courtroom scene about God's righteousness with homosexual behavior acting as a witness; Fitzmyer argues that this section portrays humanity apart from the Good News of Jesus Christ; Vines also notes the importance of this passage within scripture's message about homosexuality.[150]

Beginning with 1:18, Paul makes a case that humanity has sinned knowingly and chosen self-interest and self-fulfillment over praise and gratitude toward the Creator. Humanity rejected God; humanity rebelled against God; humanity exchanged the worship of God for the worship of itself. As a result, God allowed humanity to sink deeper into the depths of sin. Paul charges humankind with idolatry through verse 25.

Verses 26-27, continuing through the conclusion of Romans 1, illustrates the result of this idolatry. Within this theological context, homosexual behavior comes from idolatry. It also contributes to idolatry. Homosexual behavior therefore is more than just a perversion of anatomical and physical bodies. Homosexual behavior is an outward manifestation of spiritual rebellion.[151]

Sprinkle highlights Paul's phrasing here. [152] Female-female homosexual behavior is referenced here explicitly. As well, both males within male-male homosexual behavior are noted, not simply the passive partner. The terms used by Paul in 1 Corinthians 6:9 and 1 Timothy 1:10 refer literally to the passive partners within male homosexual activity [for more on this see commentary on these verses below]. Paul does not use those terms here and instead indicts both participants. This means that the sin is not related to males acting like females; it is about homosexual behavior.

Sprinkle continues. Paul has Genesis 1 and 2 in the background of these verses as the Apostle makes the case that God's intention for creation includes gender complementarity. Paul refers to homosexual behavior, of both genders, as rebellious departure from that intention. Gagnon concurs.

---

[150] Hays, *The Moral Vision of the New Testament*, 383. N. T. Wright, *Romans*, The New Interpreter's Bible, Volume 10 (Nashville: Abingdon Press, 2002), 428. Joseph A. Fitzmyer, *Romans*, The Anchor Bible (New Haven: Yale University Press, 1993), 269-270. Vines, *God and the Gay Christian: The Biblical Case in Support of Same-Sex Relationships*, 96.

[151] Fitzmyer, *Romans*, 276.

[152] Sprinkle, *People to Be Loved*, 91.

Paul has Genesis 1:26-27 in the background as he writes in Romans 1:26-27. Paul contrasts God's intended compatibility through the creation of two genders with human waywardness and descent into idolatry. Homosexuality amounts to humanity seeking to re-create God's creation.[153]

Paul uses a phrase at the conclusion of verse 26: "for unnatural ones." The Greek is *para physin*, παρὰ φύσιν. The preposition *para* denotes opposition to or against. *Physin* is "nature" or "natural order of things." Homosexuality is not in alignment with the nature of creation; it is in opposition to the natural order of things. Does Paul classify homosexual behavior as a form of human rebellion because it does not offer the possibility of procreation? Is Paul talking about gay persons with a homosexual orientation trying to live as heterosexuals and thus denying their natural urges and desires?

Vines, while acknowledging the plain sense of the verses, argues that Paul's meaning is not so obvious. Paul refers to homosexual behavior in 26b after leading that verse with a reference to shameful lust. Would Paul include monogamous same-sex relationships under the heading of shameful lusts?[154] For Vines, the answer is no. In a similar vein, Vines notes that Paul does not acknowledge nor appear to conceive of same-sex attraction and orientation. If someone was created with a sexual attraction to members of the same gender, would that person be acting *against nature* to fulfill that urge and drive or would that person be acting in accordance with their personal nature?

Vines arguments about *para physin* give one pause. However, Paul never uses *para physin* to refer to immoral forms of heterosexual intercourse. Paul utilizes other phrasing for incest, adultery and sinful heterosexual activity. Only in verse 26 does Paul use the phrase *para physin* and only in reference to homosexuality.[155]

Of note, verse 26 is the only verse within the Bible to refer to lesbians explicitly. Paul moves from female-female intercourse to male-male

---

[153] Dan Via and Gagnon, *Homosexuality and the Bible*, 79-80.

[154] Vines, *God and the Gay Christian*, 99, 103.

[155] Sprinkle, *People to Be Loved*, 97.

intercourse in the following verse. Gagnon has a point to make about this inclusion and it relates to Vines' arguments. Gagnon reads Paul's explicit reference to both types of homosexual behavior as a statement about non-exploitive homosexuality. This would include voluntary monogamous same-sex relationships as well as the homosexual orientation. Paul's expansive reference here is meant to include all reasons and forms of homosexual behavior. Gagnon argues that for Paul the orientation itself comes from humanity's sinful perversion.[156] Homosexuality in all its forms and occurrences is idolatrous and an extension of humanity's rebellion against its Creator.

Is the *para physin* of homosexuality so because homosexual activity does not have the potential of procreation, as Vines has suggested? In 1 Corinthians 7:2-5, Paul says that marriage is a means of avoiding sexual immorality. He does not state that marriage is for procreation. The *para physin* that Paul has in mind here does not relate to procreation. In fact, Paul never mentions procreation and marriage together in his writing.[157]

N.T. Wright offers Paul's logic here. Humankind mars the divine imprint that the Creator placed upon humanity. Homosexual behavior is a mechanism or instrument for distorting God's mark. Followers of Jesus—those who truly worship God—have the *imago dei* restored through grace.[158] This restoration involves understanding sinful rebellion and fleeing it in all its forms. Paul's argument advances past his illustrations of human sinfulness. As human wickedness enslaves, it is the Gospel of Jesus Christ that liberates and frees humanity, enabling God's creations to be what their Creator intended. Homosexuality does not have a place within this liberated life.

Hays notes that Paul's original readers would have understood his meaning. Paul uses homosexuality, along with other vices, to illustrate human depravity. The force of the larger theological argument is not about homosexuality per se; however, this illustration presents the Roman believers with a powerful reminder that following Jesus contrasts sharply

---

[156] Dan Via and Gagnon, *Homosexuality and the Bible*, 79-80.

[157] 1 Corinthians 7:1-41, Ephesians 5:22-33 and Colossians 3:18-4:1.

[158] Wright, *Romans*, 433-435.

with a Roman culture of sexual libertinism and homosexual behavior.[159] The Gospel makes claims on how believers live. Paul presents an expectation that followers of Christ live lives in accordance with, rather than in rebellion against, God. This includes avoiding the sin of homosexual behavior.

1 Corinthians 6:9

These verses occur within a section wherein Paul admonishes the Corinthian believers for relying upon secular courts to mediate disputes between church members. Paul presents a contrast between those who will inherit the Kingdom and those who will not. This vice list repeats the one he offered in 1 Corinthians 5:11 with several additional vices. Two of these additions concern homosexuality.

The terms malakoi, μαλακοὶ, and arsenokoitais, ἀρσενοκοίταις, occur in verse 9. Several Bible commentators argue that these terms do not refer to homosexuality. Boswell argues that malakoi should be translated as "masturbators."[160] Martin suggests translating malakoi as "effeminate."[161] He derives this through the literal meaning of malakoi, which is "soft ones." Scroggs suggests that Paul here refers to pederasty not to homosexuality.

Hays notes that malakoi is not a technical term. In Paul's day, malakoi was Greek slang for the passive partner in male intercourse.[162] This term referred to boys in pederastic relationships and male prostitutes. Sprinkle adds that the word carried connotations of men attempting to be female. Malakoi were men who were penetrated sexually.[163] Philo uses the term

---

[159] Hays, *The Moral Vision of the New Testament*, 386.

[160] John Boswell, *Christianity, Social Tolerance, and Homosexuality: Gay People in Western Europe from the Beginning of the Christian Era to the Fourteenth Century* (Chicago: University of Chicago Press, 1980), 92, 163.

[161] Dale Martin, "Arsenkoites and Malakos: Meanings and Consequences," *Biblical Ethics and Homosexuality: Listening to Scripture*, ed. Robert L. Brawley (Louisville: John Knox Press, 1996), 117.

[162] Hays, *The Moral Vision of the New Testament*, 382.

[163] Sprinkle, *People to Be Loved*, 107.

for homosexual behavior. Specifically, he refers to the feminization of receptive male partners that takes place within male homosexual intercourse.[164]

Garland asks those who say that Paul signifies pederasty here, as opposed homosexual behavior, why Paul does not utilize the Greek term for pederasty, παιδεραστία? Had Paul meant pederasty, he could have easily used this term instead of malakoi. Talbert adds that the early Christian church understood this reference to homosexual behavior, not to male prostitution nor to pederasty, in no small part because there are other terms to clearly signify an intended meaning of male prostitution or pederasty. [165] The Didache and Justin Martyr, Clement of Alexandria, Basil the Great and Chrysostom all interpret this text as referring to homosexual behavior.[166] Furthermore, in the Old Testament, the phrase "lying with a male" denoted a general concept for all forms of homosexual behavior.[167] Garland suggests translating malakoi as "those males who are sexually penetrated by males."

---

[164] Gagnon, *The Bible and Homosexual Practice*, 302.

[165] Charles Talbert, *Reading Corinthians: A Literary and Theological Commentary* (Macon, GA: Smith & Helwys, 2003), 41. Clement of Alexandria, *Exhortation to the Greeks, Book II*; Tertullian *On Modesty*; Basil, *Letters 217:62* and *The Renunciation of the World.*

[166] *The* Didache (Collegeville, MN: Liturgical Press, 2003), 5. Justin Martyr, "First Apology," *Ante-Nicene Fathers*, Volume 1, edited by Alexander Roberts and James Donaldson (Peabody, MA: Hendrickson Publishers, 1994), 172. Clement of Alexandria, "The Instructor," *Ante-Nicene Fathers*, Volume 1, edited by Alexander Roberts and James Donaldson (Peabody, MA: Hendrickson Publishers, 1994), 276-277. Basil the Great, "Letters," *Nicene and Post-Nicene Fathers*, Second Series, Volume 8, edited by Philip Schaff and Henry Wace (Peabody, MA: Hendrickson Publishers, 1994), 257. Chrysostom, "Homilies on Romans," *Nicene and Post-Nicene Fathers*, First Series, Volume 8, edited by Philip Schaff and Henry Wace (Peabody, MA: Hendrickson Publishers, 1994), 355-359.

[167] David Garland, *1 Corinthians* (Grand Rapids: Baker Academic, 2003), 213-214.

Arsenokoitais refers to male prostitutes, according to Boswell.[168] Hays asserts that this is a general term for homosexuality and not as specified as Boswell suggests. Paul utilizes a Greek version of a rabbinic phrase in writing the compound word arsenokoitais.[169] Arsenokoitais is not used in any existing Greek text outside of 1 Corinthians 6:9 and 1 Timothy 1:10. It comes from a combination of words used in the Septuagint translation of Leviticus 20:13. The Hebrew phrase mishkab zakur, זָכָר֙ מִשְׁכְּבֵ֣י, describes male homosexual behavior. The LXX version of this phrase is ἄρσενος κοίτην, arsenos koiten.[170] Given this correspondence, Paul intended arsenokoitais to refer to homosexual behavior, not male prostitution, linking verse 9 with the Levitical prohibitions in chapters 18 and 20.

Paul affirmed the Holiness Code regarding homosexuality. His use of an imprecise term malakoi and a word derived from the Greek translation of Hebrew in Leviticus makes the point that he expected his readers to understand his meaning. The original readers read a prohibition of homosexual behavior in 1 Corinthians 6:9. Paul's intended meaning has not changed over 2000 years.

1 Timothy 1:10

This section corresponds to those who break the law. Paul writes to oppose false teachers of the gospel, seeking to offer guidance to Timothy. The law is intended to secure the community by restraining vice. Oden notes that the thrust of the passage, verses 3-11, makes the argument that godly living comes as an implication of the Gospel.[171] Those that know Christ will not act unrighteously.

---

[168] John Boswell, *Christianity, Social Tolerance, and Homosexuality: Gay People in Western Europe from the Beginning of the Christian Era to the Fourteenth Century*, 333.

[169] Robert Hays, *First Corinthians*, Interpretation: A Bible Commentary for Teaching and Preaching (Louisville: John Knox Press, 2011), 97.

[170] Gagnon, *The Bible and Homosexual Practice*, 67.

[171] Thomas C. Oden, *First and Second Timothy, Titus*, Interpretation: A Bible Commentary for Teaching and Preaching (Atlanta: John Knox Press, 1989), 41.

Paul again uses the Greek word arsenokoitais, ἀρσενοκοίταις, to refer to homosexuals. The reference occurs within the vice list of verses 9-10. Within this vice list, homosexuality seems to stand aside from other forms of sexual immorality. It appears as a different category of sexual sin. The larger category for Paul, including other vices, is anything against sound teaching. This makes the basis for the prohibition theological, not sociological or psychological. Homosexual behavior exhibits bad theology.

Hays argues that this verse for Paul presupposes the Holiness Code prohibitions in Leviticus.[172] Paul is in line with Jewish thought as he provides counsel for the early Christian church. Both Sprinkle and Gagnon argue that this verse reinforces both Paul's terminology usage and intended meaning in 1 Corinthians 6:9.[173] Here, Paul is consistent with both Judaism and his other pronouncements on homosexual practice. His words call the church to consistent truth as well.

Consistent truth comes from the Gospel. Refraining from crime, murder, perversion, homosexuality, enslavement and blasphemy occurs naturally for the Christian.[174] Solid teaching is a result of faith. Living according to that sound doctrine is both an expectation of believers and a consequence of the relationship between those believers and Jesus Christ.

---

[172] Hays, *The Moral Vision of the New Testament*, 383.

[173] Sprinkle, *People to be Loved: Why Homosexuality is Not Just an Issue*, 117. Gagnon, *The Bible and Homosexual Practice*, 332.

[174] James D. G. Dunn, *1 Timothy*, The New Interpreter's Bible: Second Corinthians – Philemon, Volume 11 (Nashville: Abingdon Press, 2000), 792.

APPENDIX B

ABCO FLASH Church Survey

Please respond to the following items using the scale: 1) strongly disagree, 2) disagree, 3) neither disagree nor agree, 4) agree, 5) strongly agree.

1. My church has gay/lesbian persons attending services.____
2. My church would baptize a celibate gay/lesbian person.___
3. My church would baptize a non-celibate gay/lesbian person.______
4. My church would allow a celibate gay/lesbian person to become a congregation member._____
5. My church would allow a non-celibate gay/lesbian person to become a congregation member._____
6. My church would hold a dedication service for the adopted or biological child of a gay/lesbian couple.______
7. My church would allow a celibate gay/lesbian person to serve as a church volunteer, such as participate in choir._____
8. My church would allow a non-celibate gay/lesbian person to serve as a church volunteer, such as participate in choir._____
9. My church would allow a celibate gay/lesbian person to serve in church leadership, such as an elected board member._____
10. My church would allow a non-celibate gay/lesbian person to serve in church leadership, such as an elected board member.____
11. My church would allow a staff member to conduct a gay/lesbian wedding.___
12. My church would host a gay/lesbian wedding._______

Please answer the following questions in the textboxes provided.

13. How would you characterize your church's position on homosexuality?

14. How did your church arrive at this position?

15. How has this position been communicated internally within the church?

16. How has this position been communicated externally outside of the church?

17. What has been the greatest difficulty within your congregation surrounding homosexuality?

APPENDIX C

First Baptist Church Scottsdale, Arizona Survey

Please respond to the following items using the scale: 1) strongly disagree, 2) disagree, 3) neither disagree nor agree, 4) agree, 5) strongly agree.

1. First Baptist Church, Scottsdale, Arizona, has gay/lesbian persons attending services.____
2. First Baptist Church, Scottsdale, Arizona, would baptize a celibate gay/lesbian person.____
3. First Baptist Church, Scottsdale, Arizona, would baptize a non-celibate gay/lesbian person.___
4. First Baptist Church, Scottsdale, Arizona, would allow a celibate gay/lesbian person to become a congregation member.______
5. First Baptist Church, Scottsdale, Arizona, would allow a non-celibate gay/lesbian person to become a congregation member. ______
6. First Baptist Church, Scottsdale, Arizona, would hold a dedication service for the adopted or biological child of a gay/lesbian couple. ______

7. First Baptist Church, Scottsdale, Arizona, would allow a gay/lesbian person to serve as a church volunteer, such as participate in choir.________

8. First Baptist Church, Scottsdale, Arizona, would allow a celibate gay/lesbian person to serve in church leadership, such as an elected board member.______

9. First Baptist Church, Scottsdale, Arizona, would allow a staff member to conduct a gay/lesbian wedding.___

10. First Baptist Church, Scottsdale, Arizona, would host a gay/lesbian wedding._____

11. A gay person would be welcome at First Baptist Church, Scottsdale, Arizona,._____

12. A gay person would be welcome at any Worship Service at First Baptist Church, Scottsdale, Arizona,.________

13. A gay person would be welcome at any Grow Group at First Baptist Church, Scottsdale, Arizona,.________

14. A gay person would be welcome at any Serve Team at First Baptist Church, Scottsdale, Arizona,.________

15. I would invite a gay friend/neighbor/co-worker to First Baptist Church, Scottsdale, Arizona,.________

16. I do not see any hindrances to a gay person feeling welcomed at First Baptist Church, Scottsdale, Arizona,.____

Please answer the following questions in the space provided.

17. How would you characterize First Baptist Church, Scottsdale, Arizona,'s position on homosexuality?

18. What has been the greatest difficulty within First Baptist Church, Scottsdale, Arizona, surrounding homosexuality?

19. How might First Baptist Church, Scottsdale, Arizona, offer hospitality to a gay person?

20. How might you offer hospitality to a gay person?

21. What makes First Baptist Church, Scottsdale, Arizona, hospitable to gay persons?

22. What hinders gay persons from finding hospitality at First Baptist Church, Scottsdale, Arizona,?

Initials:________________

These surveys will be kept confidential until the completion of the study at which time they will be shredded.

BIBLIOGRAPHY

Aristotle, *Nicomachean Ethics,* Trans. C. D. C. Reeve. Indianapolis: Hackett Publishing Co. Inc., 2014.

Bailey, Kenneth. *Poet and Peasant and Through Peasant Eyes: A Literary-Cultural Approach to the Parables in* Luke, combined edition. Grand Rapids: Eerdmans, 1983.

Barth, Karl. *Church Dogmatics IV/1.* Eugene, OR: Wipf & Stock Publishers, 2001.

———. *Church Dogmatics III/1.* Edinburgh: T & T Clark, 1958.

Basil the Great, "Letters," *Nicene and Post-Nicene Fathers*, Second Series, Volume 8. Edited by Philip Schaff and Henry Wace. Peabody, MA: Hendrickson Publishers, 1994.

Boswell, John. *Christianity, Social Tolerance, and Homosexuality: Gay People in Western Europe from the Beginning of the Christian Era to the Fourteenth Century*. Chicago: University of Chicago Press, 1980.

Breidenthal, Thomas. "Sanctifying Nearness." *Theology and Sexuality: Classic and Contemporary Readings*. Edited by Eugene Rogers. Malden, MA: Blackwell Publishers, 2002.

Brownson, James. *Bible Gender Sexuality: Reframing the Church's Debate on Same-Sex Relationships*. Grand Rapids: Eerdmans, 2013.

Brueggemann, Walter. *Genesis*, Interpretation: A Bible Commentary for Teaching and Preaching. Atlanta: John Knox Press, 1982.

Burk, Denny, and Heath Lambert. *Transforming Homosexuality: What the Bible Says about Sexual Orientation and Change*. Phillipsburg, NJ: P&R Publishing, 2015.

Chrysostom, "Homilies on Romans," *Nicene and Post-Nicene Fathers*, First Series, Volume 8. Edited by Philip Schaff and Henry Wace. Peabody, MA: Hendrickson Publishers, 1994.

Clement of Alexandria, "The Instructor," *Ante-Nicene Fathers*, Volume 1. Edited by Alexander Roberts and James Donaldson. Peabody, MA: Hendrickson Publishers, 1994.

Coles, Gregory. *Single Gay Christian: A Personal Journey of Faith and Sexual Identity*. Downers Grove: IVP Books, 2017.

Collins, Nate. *All but Invisible: Exploring Identity Questions at the Intersection of Faith, Gender & Sexuality*. Grand Rapids: Zondervan, 2017.

The Didache. Collegeville, MN: Liturgical Press, 2003.

Dowd, Sharyn. *Reading Mark: A Literary and Theological Commentary on the Second Gospel*, Reading the New Testament, Vol. 2. Macon, GA: Smyth & Helwys Publishing, 2000.

Dunn, James D. G. *1 Timothy*. The New Interpreter's Bible: Second Corinthians – Philemon, Vol. 11. Nashville: Abingdon Press, 2000.

Evdokimov, Paul. "The Sacrament of Love: The Nuptial Mystery in the Light of Orthodox Tradition." *Theology and Sexuality: Classic and Contemporary Readings*. Edited by Eugene Rogers. Malden, MA: Blackwell Publishers, 2002.

Fitzmyer, Joseph A. *The Gospel According to Luke X-XXIV: Introduction, Translation and Notes*, The Anchor Bible, vols. 2, 28. New York: Doubleday & Co., 1985.

———. *Romans*. The Anchor Bible. New Haven: Yale University Press, 1993.

Fretheim, Terence. *The Book of Genesis*. The New Interpreter's Bible, Vol. 1. Nashville: Abingdon Press, 1994.

Furnish, Victor. *The Moral Teaching of Paul*. Nashville: Abingdon Press, 2009.

Gagnon, Robert. *The Bible and Homosexual Practice*. Nashville: Abingdon Press, 2002.

Garland, David. *1 Corinthians*. Grand Rapids: Baker Academic, 2003.

———. *Luke*. Zondervan Exegetical Commentary on the New Testament. Grand Rapids: Zondervan, 2011.

Grant, Jonathan. *Divine Sex: A Compelling Vision for Christian Relationships in a Hypersexualized Age*. Grand Rapids: Brazos Press, 2015.

Green, Michael. *Evangelism in the Early Church*. Grand Rapids: Eerdmans, 2003.

Grenz, Stanley. *Welcoming but Not Affirming*. Louisville: Westminster John Knox Press, 1998.

Gushee, David P. *Changing Our Mind*, 2nd Edition. Canton, MI: Read the Spirit Books, 2015.

Hamilton, Victor P. *The Book of Genesis: Chapters 1-17*. NICOT. Grand Rapids: Eerdmans, 1990.

———. *The Book of Genesis: Chapters 18-50*. NICOT. Grand Rapids: Eerdmans, 1995.

Hauerwas, Stanley. "Gay Friendship: A Thought Experiment." *Theology and Sexuality: Classic and Contemporary Readings*. Edited by Eugene Rogers. Malden, MA: Blackwell Publishers, 2002.

Hays, Richard. *First Corinthians*. Interpretation: A Bible Commentary for Teaching and Preaching. Louisville: John Knox Press, 2011.

———. *The Moral Vision of the New Testament*. San Francisco: Harper, 1996.

Hill, Wesley. *Spiritual Friendship: Finding Love in the Church as a Celibate Gay*. Grand Rapids: Brazos Press, 2015.

———. *Washed and Waiting: Reflections on Christian Faithfulness and Homosexuality*. Grand Rapids: Zondervan, 2010.

Hirsch, Debra. *Redeeming Sex: Naked Conversations about Sexuality and Spirituality.* Downers Grove: IVP Books, 2015.

Hubbard, Thomas K., *Homosexuality in Greece and Rome: A Sourcebook of Basic Documents*. Berkeley: University of California Press, 2003.

Hurtado, Larry W. *Mark.* Understanding the Bible Commentary Series, vol. 2. Ada, MI: Baker Books, 1989.

Jeremias, Joachim. *New Testament Theology: The Proclamation of Jesus*. New York: Scribner, 1971.

Johnson, Luke Timothy. "Disputed Questions: Debate and Discernment, Scripture and Spirit." *Theology and Sexuality: Classic and Contemporary Readings*. Edited by Eugene Rogers. Malden, MA: Blackwell Publishers, 2002.

Kaiser, Walter C., Jr. *Leviticus*, New Interpreter's Bible: Genesis to Leviticus, Vol. 1. Nashville: Abingdon Press, 1994.

Lee, Justin. *Torn: Rescuing the Gospel from the Gays vs. Christians Debate*. Nashville: Jericho Books, 2013.

Lewis, Clive Staples, *The Four Loves,* NY: Harcourt Brace Jovanovich, 1960.

Loader, William. *Making Sense of Sex: Attitudes towards Sexuality in Early Jewish and Christian Literature*. Grand Rapids: Eerdmans, 2013.

———. The *New Testament on Sexuality*. Grand Rapids: Eerdmans, 2012.

———. *Sexuality and the Jesus Tradition*. Grand Rapids: Eerdmans, 2005.

Marin, Andrew. *Love Is an Orientation: Elevating the Conversation with the Gay Community*. Downers Grove: IVP Books, 2009.

———. "Arsenkoites and Malakos: Meanings and Consequences." *Biblical Ethics and Homosexuality: Listening to Scripture*. Edited by Robert L. Brawley. Louisville: John Knox Press, 1996.

Martyr, Justin, "First Apology," *Ante-Nicene Fathers*, Volume 1. Edited by Alexander Roberts and James Donaldson. Peabody, MA: Hendrickson Publishers, 1994.

Moltmann, Jurgen, *The Spirit of Life: A Universal Affirmation*, Minneapolis: Fortress Press, 1992.

Newman, Elizabeth. *Untamed Hospitality: Welcoming God and Other Strangers*. Grand Rapids: Brazos Press, 2007.

Niebuhr, H. Richard *The Kingdom of God in America*. Fishers, IN: Wesleyan, 1988.

Oden, Amy G. *And You Welcomed Me: A Sourcebook on Hospitality in Early Christianity*. Nashville: Abingdon Press, 2001.

———. *God's Welcome: Hospitality for a Gospel-Hungry World.* Cleveland: Pilgrim Press, 2008.

Oden, Thomas C. *First and Second Timothy, Titus*. Interpretation: A Bible Commentary for Teaching and Preaching. Atlanta: John Knox Press, 1989.

Parker, Palmer. *The Company of Strangers: Christians and the Renewal of America's Public Life*. New York: The Crossroad Publishing Company, 1983.

Plato, "Symposium," in *Plato: Collected Dialogues,* edited by Edith Hamilton and Huntington Cairns. Princeton: Princeton UP, 1989.

Plutarch, "Dialogue on Love," *On Love, the Family and the Good Life: Selected Essays of Plutarch*, edited by Moses Hadas. Ann Arbor: University of Michigan, 1957.

Pohl, Christine D. *Making Room: Recovering Hospitality as a Christian Tradition*. Grand Rapids: Eerdmans Publishing Company, 1999.

Pseudo-Clementine. "Recognitions of Clement." In *Ante-Nicene Fathers*, Vol. 8. Peabody, MA: Hendrickson Publishers, 1994.

Rogers, Eugene, ed. *Theology and Sexuality: Classic and Contemporary Readings*. Malden, MA: Blackwell Publishers, 2002.

Rorty, Richard. *Everything Belongs: The Gift of Contemplative Prayer*. NY: Crossroad, 2003.

Schmidt, Thomas E. *Straight & Narrow? Compassion & Clarity in the Homosexuality Debate.* Downers Grove: IVP Books, 1995.

Scroggs, Robin. *The Text and the Times: New Testament Essays for Today.* Minneapolis: Fortress Press, 1993.

———. *New Testament and Homosexuality*. Philadelphia: Fortress Press, 1983.

Song, Robert. *Covenant and Calling: Towards a Theology of Same-Sex Relationships*. London: SCM Press, 2014.

Sprinkle, Preston, ed. *Two Views on Homosexuality, the Bible and the Church*, Counterpoints Bible & Theology. Grand Rapids: Zondervan, 2016.

———. *People to Be Loved: Why Homosexuality is Not Just an Issue*. Grand Rapids: Zondervan, 2015.

Stark, Rodney. *The Rise of Christianity.* San Francisco: Harper, 1997.

Talbert, Charles. *Reading Corinthians: A Literary and Theological Commentary*. Macon, GA: Smith & Helwys, 2003.

Tertullian. "Apology." *Ante-Nicene Fathers*, Vol. 3. Peabody, MA: Hendrickson Publishers, 1994.

Thompson, Chad. *Loving Homosexuals as Jesus Would.* Grand Rapids: Brazos Press, 2004.

Vanier, Jean. *Community and Growth.* New York: Paulist Press, 1989.

———. *Encountering the Other*. New York: Paulist Press, 2006.

———. *From Brokenness to Community*. New York: Paulist Press, 1992.

Via, Dan, and Robert Gagnon. *Homosexuality and the Bible: Two Views.* Minneapolis: Augsburg Fortress, 2009.

Vines, Matthew. *God and the Gay Christian: The Biblical Case in Support of Same-Sex Relationships*. New York: Convergent Books, 2015.

Vogt, W. Paul, Dianne C. Gardner, and Lynne M. Haeffele. *When to Use What Research Design*. New York: The Guilford Press, 2012.

Volf, Mirolsav. "'The Trinity is Our Social Program': The Doctrine of the Trinity and the Shape of Social Engagement." *Modern Theology* 14, No. 3 (July 1998): 403-423.

———. *Exclusion and Embrace: A Theological Exploration of Identity, Otherness and Reconciliation* (Nashville: Abingdon Press, 1996).

Webb, William J. *Slaves, Women & Homosexuals: Exploring the Hermeneutics of Cultural Analysis*. Downers Grove: IVP Books, 2001.

Webster, John. *Holiness*. Grand Rapids: Eerdmans, 2003.

Williams, Rowan. "The Body's Grace." *Theology and Sexuality: Classic and Contemporary Readings*. Edited by Eugene Rogers. Malden, MA: Blackwell Publishers, 2002.

Wilson, Ken. *A Letter to My Congregation*. Canton, MI: Read the Spirit Books, 2014.

Witherington, Ben, III. *The Rest of Life: Rest, Play, Eating, Studying, Sex from a Kingdom Perspective*. Grand Rapids: Eerdmans, 2012.

Wright, N. T. *Romans*. The New Interpreter's Bible, Vol. 10. Nashville: Abingdon Press, 2002.

James H. Coston is available for interviews. For more information email:

info@advbooks.com

To purchase additional copies of these books, visit our bookstore at:
www.advbookstore.com

Orlando, Florida, USA
"we bring dreams to life"™
www.advbookstore.com

www.ingramcontent.com/pod-product-compliance
Lightning Source LLC
Chambersburg PA
CBHW051720090426
42738CB00010B/2010

* 9 7 8 1 5 9 7 5 5 7 1 8 4 *